PARAPSYCHOLOGICAL RESEARCH WITH CHILDREN:

An Annotated Bibliography

by

ATHENA A. DREWES

and

SALLY ANN DRUCKER

The Scarecrow Press, Inc.
Metuchen, N.J., & London
1991

British Library Cataloguing-in-Publication data available

Library of Congress Cataloging-in-Publication Data

Drewes, Athena A., 1948-
Parapsychological research with children : an annotated bibliography / by Athena A. Drewes and Sally Ann Drucker.
p. cm.
Includes six papers presented at the Thirty-third Parapsychological Association Convention, Washington, DC, Aug. 17-20, 1990.
Includes index.
ISBN 0-8108-2514-7 (alk. paper)
1. Children--Psychic ability--Bibliography. 2. Parapsychology--Bibliography. 3. Children--Psychic ability. I. Drucker, Sally Ann. II. Parapsychological Association. Convention (33rd : 1990 : Washington, D.C.). III. Title.
Z6878.P8D64 1991
[BF1045.C45]
133.8'088054--dc20 91-39046

Manufactured in the United States of America

Printed on acid-free paper

This book is dedicated

to my sons, Scott Richard Drewes Bridges
and Seth Andrew Bridges,

to Helen Novicker Drucker (1911-1985),
whose interest in psychic phenomena
inspired her daughter's,

and to the child within us all.

ACKNOWLEDGMENTS

We wish to extend our appreciation to the Newburgh Free Library, to the Parapsychology Foundation, to the Foundation for Research on the Nature of Man/Institute for Parapsychology, and to the staffs of these organizations, for their support of this endeavor. The continual availability of library materials has made the extensive researching of this book more manageable.

As in all works of creation, many people have been instrumental by contributing in various ways, from their abundant support to the submission of additional materials and references. We gratefully thank Charles Honorton, Laura Dale, Marian Nester, Fannie Knipe, Rhea White, Katie Donnelly, Charles and Mariko Drewes, Lynn Kelly, and Janet Mitchell for their special contributions and never-ending interest. There is a very special heartfelt thanks to James Richard Bridges for his endless statistical consultations, pointed editorial comments, and overall emotional availability and support.

James G. Matlock contributed a large portion of the entries in the Reincarnation section. We thank him for this and for his ongoing interest in and generous help with the project. We are grateful for his willingness to share his expertise.

This book was computer-set and prepared for printing by Max Drucker, whose fifty years of experience in book production greatly aided our work. We thank him for the time and energy he put into formatting, word-processing, and proofreading.

CONTENTS

FOREWORD

John Palmer, Ph.D.

Foundation for Research on the Nature of Man
Durham, NC

In 1979, I published a random mail survey of psychic experiences among residents of Charlottesville, Virginia. About half of the respondents claimed to have had at least one spontaneous ESP experience in their lifetime. As a professional parapsychologist, I frequently receive phone calls from people all over the country who are troubled by spontaneous ESP experiences, apparitions, or poltergeist outbreaks. Occasionally these people are mentally ill, but many seem to be well-adjusted individuals holding down responsible jobs and quite capable of dealing with their experiences rationally and objectively. Although many people seem able to cope easily with occasional psi experiences, our phone callers invariably want the experiences to stop. After running through the usual list of nonparapsychological explanations, there is little I can do but reassure them that other people have these experiences as well. Mental health professionals often don't know how to help these people either, and on a few occasions I have had them, in effect, refer their patients to me.

The preceding paragraph might seem an odd way to introduce a book on basic research about psychic phenomena in children. I did so to make the point that parapsychological research is more than an ivory tower exercise. Our inability to help people troubled by unwanted psychic experiences is partly attributable to our lack of a basic understanding not only of the experiences per se but also of the genuine paranormal processes that I believe underlie many of them. The latter is what parapsychology is all about. Only through scientific understanding will we reach the point where people can control psi rather than having psi control them.

For better or worse, much psi research, and certainly the most well-known psi research, is directed toward proving the very reality of psychic phenomena to a skeptical scientific community. This objective has yet to be achieved, despite a growing body of well-controlled research that even some critics of the field concede is not subject to plausible conventional interpretations. At the very least, this body of research should suggest to objective observers that there is a substantial probability that paranormal processes do sometimes occur, and not just in high-profile "psychics." Other psi research has begun with the premise that paranormal processes are real and has tried to understand them. Theories have evolved attempting to relate psi to such diverse conceptual systems as quantum theory in physics and reinforcement theory in psychology. Research has been undertaken to find out what kinds of people score best on tests of psi and what test conditions seem most conducive to psi. There is also a small but hopefully growing body of research devoted to studying real-life psi experiences from theoretical perspectives.

This finally brings me to psi research with children. Most of the findings in psi research, including those alluded to above, have come from studying adults. Although there has been some research with children -- just about all of which is cited in this book -- it represents only a small percentage of research in the field as a whole. This is attributable partly to the fact that only a handful of parapsychologists have the special skills needed to conduct research with children, particularly young ones. Yet children are a most promising population for parapsychologists to study. What little we know about psi suggests that paranormal processes are inhibited by intellectual development and enculturation. Successful techniques for enhancing psi performance in adults, such as the ganzfeld (a short-term sensory deprivation procedure) and hypnosis, seem to work in part by shutting off higher mental processes and removing subjects' normal cultural bearings. Although I would not wish to be interpreted too literally here, these techniques are somewhat analogous to regressing adults to a more childlike state. If this reasoning is anywhere close to the mark, there is a case to be made for using participants who are already in a childlike state -- children!

The psi research conducted so far with children has provided some encouraging results. Future research in the area will do well to draw heavily on knowledge acquired in the broader field of developmental psychology, both methodologically and theoretically. The following compendium of what has happened to date in what might be dubbed developmental parapsychology will be valuable both to future researchers in this area and to the general reader who is interested in children and psi.

INTRODUCTION

Sometimes, young children seem to pick up on their parents' thoughts. For instance, a child names what will be cooked for dinner that night, or whom the parent is thinking of calling. Some examples of a child's psychic abilities are even more dramatic.

For three weeks, a six-year-old boy has nightmares about "falling in a hole." Playing in his neighbor's yard, where there is still snow on the ground, he falls into the hole of an old septic tank and is in water up to his shoulders before he is rescued.

A girl, almost five, always knows what Christmas gifts have been bought for her ("my little blue purse") and correctly predicts when relatives will come to visit, although her mother thinks these visits impossible. When her father is ill, she correctly describes when his blood transfusions stop, when he is first given food, and when he first walks to the window. She predicts that he will recover, despite the opinion of experts. Her father recovers. The girl also does extraordinarily well on card-guessing ESP tests administered by her mother.

The above cases are cited in Louisa E. Rhine's Hidden Channels of the Mind. They were culled from many psi events involving children that were sent to what was then Duke University's Parapsychology Laboratory (now the Foundation for Research on the Nature of Man, an independent institute).

Some unusual types of spontaneous psi, such as poltergeist phenomena, hauntings, and past life memory (reincarnation) cases also involve children. Certainly, both in common experience and in the literature of parapsychology, there is enough material to justify the large amount of experimental work that has focused on children.

Until now, however, there has been no extensive annotated bibliography on the parapsychological phenomena associated with children. Researchers, teachers, students, therapists, parents, and all others interested in parapsychological work done with children have had to depend on hit or miss reading, references from previously published pieces, shorter or unannotated bibliographies, or surveys dealing with one aspect of children's ESP only, such as classroom experiments (Van de Castle, 1959; White & Angstadt, 1961, 1965) or reincarnation cases (Stevenson, 1987).

For all other research areas involving children's ESP, information has been spotty and sometimes hard to find, at times published in non-parapsychological journals. Usually, popular books and articles on psychic children have not been research oriented, or else focus on individual cases. Yet, there are several areas of parapsychological research in which children are central, such as the above-mentioned classroom experiments. Also, children have shown ESP ability in the same general areas that adults have: telepathy, precognition, clairvoyance, and psychokinesis.

For researchers, a problem in working with children has been consolidating what was already known, having an overview as a key to envisioning further research. When we began our experiments with very young children, ages four through eight (Drucker & Rubin, 1975; Drucker & Drewes, 1976; Drucker, Drewes, & Rubin, 1977; Drewes & Drucker, 1977), we encountered this problem and wished that someone had written a bibliography of research done on children's ESP. Also, we were often asked where people could go for information on psi in children, once people knew we were doing that type of research. This bibliography grew out of our research. We hope that it will encourage others to work with children, since many studies have never been replicated and new areas remain open to exploration.

Testing Children

The following guidelines should be of use to researchers interested in parapsychological testing involving children. With some modifications, parents and teachers can use these guidelines as well.

Parapsychological research with children can be challenging, yet fun and productive, if approached with some basic understanding of children and their needs. Children often make excellent subjects. They are not yet accepting of our cultural concepts of what is possible or impossible, are not negatively conditioned about psychic phenomena, and, especially when younger, have a less structured and limited concept of time. While many researchers are afraid to work with children as subjects, a review of the literature shows that it can be done successfully if special test requirements are met. In fact, children are sometimes better subjects in experiments than are adults (Bottrill, 1969).

Establishing rapport, making the tasks playful, interesting, and colorful, and gearing the test to the child's cognitive level are essential components for testing children. Maintaining rapport with a child subject is important. Some people may find they are comfortable in working with children, either from their own experiences or a general interest in this area. Others may not feel so comfortable. They will need to learn, or perhaps relearn, how best to relate to children. Children who are cooperative or obedient will present few problems. The researcher just needs to explain what is to be done and these children will readily agree to try whatever the experimenter requires of them. It will take more effort to engage the child who may be shy or has limited verbal abilities.

Both shy and outgoing children may enter new situations with caution and wariness. The experimenter must be attuned to their feelings and needs as individuals. The experimenter should try to put the child at ease. Casual conversation about favorite TV shows, pets, hobbies, or activities can help ease into a testing situation. Using some readily accessible toys like cars and blocks, or having the child draw pictures of favorite animals or scenes, can help ease discomfort and maximize performance by allowing the child some initial control over the situation. Some children may find the testing stressful, regardless of your attempts. With these children, it is best to acknowledge their discomfort verbally and to terminate the session. Sometimes, this is enough for the child to want to resume the activity or have the motivation to try; however, there may be times when the child will accept your offer to stop. In this case, an opportunity to try again at a later date could be offered.

It is important to be honest and direct when trying to elicit a child's cooperation. Children come to the research situation with varying degrees of preparation. The experimenter should not assume that the child will experience exactly what the parent initially described to the child. A brief, accurate description of why you and the child are working together is important. The extent of the explanation will depend upon the child's cognitive level of understanding. Children of all ages, even preschoolers, are aware of testing and adult expectations, regardless of how you describe your experiment. They are aware of their misses and failures, as well as possible subtle cues from the experimenter. It is best to inform them honestly that they will not be able to succeed on every item but that the goal is to see how well they can do. Constant encouragement and praise while the child performs the experiment can alleviate anxiety about not doing well and helps to maintain his or her interest. Actively engaging the child in the experiment through tangible or edible rewards for correct guesses, or by helping the experimenter turn pages, increases the child's motivation and lessens his/her anxiety.

Instructions should be clear and specific to the immediate task. Some children will say they understand, when in fact, they may be embarrassed to indicate otherwise. The experimenter should be sensitive to any uneasiness a child may show and explore it to deal with any misunderstandings or needs (such as a trip to the bathroom). Setting the emotional tone of the experimental situation is very important; it should be comfortable and not distracting. Enlisting parental cooperation and enthusiasm, figuring out what to do with siblings if the experiment is done in the home, and making sure the environment is peaceful and relaxed in every way are all desirable. Proper lighting and comfortable seating geared toward children are strongly advised. Because very young children have short attention spans, the length of the trial or session needs to be considered. Several short trials can be better than one long one.

While children may in many ways be ideal subjects, a note of caution is necessary. As with any subject pool, young people will sometimes engage in fraudulent test behavior. As far back as 1848 during the Spiritualism era, the Fox children's skills as psychic mediums came under question. Since that time, there have been numerous cases of children committing fraud in the field of psychical research (Nicol, 1979). In more recent years, there has been skepticism about the abilities of mini-Gellers, children who seem to have abilities to bend metal objects in imitation of Uri Geller, an Israeli performer alleged to possess psychokinetic abilities. Delanoy (1987) has reported on a fraudulent case of PK metal-bending with a 17-year-old subject. The difficulties of setting up and maintaining adequate controls during experiments, especially those experiments dealing with PK, contribute to the possibilities of both intentional and unintentional deception. Added pressure to succeed can occur because children seek adult approval and may enjoy the attention they receive for their performance. What might have originated as an authentic psychic phenomenon may become forced and fraudulent with repeated, on-demand performances. Since psychic abilities often wax and wane, depending upon who the experimenter is, and the mood, physical state, and motivation of the subject, it seems very likely that some child subjects may try to enhance their scores artificially, so as not to disappoint others or lose the attention they have begun to enjoy. Therefore, researchers should consider the possibility of fraud when designing studies with children, so that adequate controls and safeguards are imposed.

Cognitive and Developmental Considerations

The child's level of cognitive thinking needs to be considered when devising ESP experiments. Piaget has four developmental periods of cognitive thinking: 1) the sensorimotor stage, birth to two years; 2) the preoperational stage, two to six years; 3) the stage of concrete operations, six to twelve years; and 4) the stage of formal operations, which continues from adolescence into adulthood.

In the sensorimotor stage (birth to two years) the symbiotic mother-child relationship is of critical importance (Ehrenwald, 1971). Several ESP studies have utilized this factor in formulating research. Fisk (1951-1952) obtained significant clairvoyant results with a 14-month-old girl, and Bierman (1985) worked with 10-month-old infants using computer-generated video displays of a laughing face. During the preoperational stage (2-6 years) the child deals with the world in a more realistic way. Curiosity and excitement are high. Although vocabulary development is rapidly growing, during this stage, a child still has limited verbal skills. Thinking will tend to be accessible more through nonverbal than verbal means. Thinking will be intuitive, imaginative, determined by magical and animal beliefs, and unrestrained by adult logical rules. Drucker, Drewes, & Rubin (1977) used colorful M & M candies as targets with children ages 4 to 7. Creative cards using dogs, cats, fish, and boats as test targets were used by Krippner (1965).

Children in the concrete operational stage (6-12 years) think more concretely and less intuitively than during the previous stage. They become more rational and more concerned with categories of objects. Although they can begin to plan ahead, often they will quickly tackle a problem; their approach will be practical based on empirical evidence. Kanthamani, Khilji, and Perlstrom (1985) used specially designed target decks with cartoon characters. Rewards of stickers aided in their motivational experiment with children ages 5 to 10. Winkelman (1981) used small monetary awards and candy incentives in psi tests with 8 to 14-year-olds. Targets were red, green, and yellow candies, and colored marbles, for use in clairvoyance, PK, and precognition tests. Anderson (1960) had 8 to 12-year-olds launch a mythical missile. Tornatore (1983) utilized a fantasy scenario using E. T., the extraterrestrial from the popular movie, to aid in telepathic communication among second graders.

The fourth stage, formal operations, begins in early puberty and continues into adulthood. The adolescent's thinking makes a significant shift from a concrete to an abstract level. Here and now concerns give way to a speculative stance, examining the whole situation and considering what the possibilities, connections, and alternatives are. Thinking is now on a higher order. There is an intricate interplay of memory, imagination, processing information, drawing inferences, and flexibly making choices. Consequently, the types of ESP testing for this stage become more elaborate. Studies become more involved with correlations between ESP and personality variables, attitudes, and/or beliefs (Haight,1979; Krishna and Rao, 1980; and Blackmore and Troscianko, 1985). With this age group, researchers have examined conditions of competition and cooperation with same- and opposite-sex pairs (Rao and Kanthamani, 1981), as well as attempts to use psychokinetic abilities on fluids and metals (Egely, 1985; and Hasted, 1977).

Parents as well as researchers wonder about the relationship of children's ESP to developmental patterns. Many spontaneous cases have been reported for the earliest years of life. The symbiotic mother-child relationship, from prebirth to about age two, is of crucial importance. In addition, numerous psi interactions have been reported for the preschool child once he or she begins to speak clearly. Although in our culture spontaneous ESP ability appears to diminish greatly at the age that children enter school, the classroom ESP studies show that various factors (such as time of the school year, sex of the teacher and student, rapport between teacher and student, age of the student in relation to test type) can heighten the response. Work relating ESP to IQ is not yet conclusive (Drucker, Drewes, & Rubin, 1977). In all test situations with children, as with those involving adults, personality differences between children affect scoring; "believers" in ESP score higher than "nonbelievers" (Musso, 1965), and withdrawn children score lower than nonwithdrawn (Shields, 1962; Shields & Mulders, 1975). Poltergeist phenomena seem to center around a child at puberty or adolescence, or a young adult with adolescent conflicts. The presence of the phenomena often indicate major problems within the individual or within a dysfunctional family situation.

Parents often want to know how to handle a child's ESP. The most positive thing that a parent can do is to give relaxed encouragement, treating the child as neither a freak nor a superpsychic. Keeping a journal of spontaneous ESP phenomena to note trends (Schwarz, 1961, 1971), encouraging the child to talk about his or her dreams, playing ESP guessing games now and then, giving an older child books on parapsychology -- all these activities can be both fun and learning experiences for the child. Also, the more knowledgeable the parent is about how ESP phenomena appear in children, the easier it is to interpret specific cases. We hope that this bibliography will aid not only researchers, but also parents and others interested in children's ESP.

Components of the Book

Our bibliography covers over 100 years of research, with articles spanning from the 1880s up to 1990, testifying to ongoing interest in children's ESP. It is organized to include all parapsychological research conducted with children age 17 and under appearing in parapsychological and nonparapsychological journals, published in the United States and other countries. (See **Journals** listings.) Spontaneous cases, popular books or articles, and book reviews are also included where relevant. The first three chapters of the bibliography cover studies of children's ESP in the major research areas of **Clairvoyance, Telepathy,** and **Precognition.** Because of the large number of studies covered, these chapters are further subdivided into Pre-school/elementary age (infancy to 12 years), Junior high schoolers (13 to 15 years), and High schoolers (15 to 17 years). The subdivisions should aid the reader in finding research relating to a particular age group. Because of a smaller number of cases, the fourth area of research, **Psychokinesis,** is not similarly subdivided. The fifth and sixth chapters, **Poltergeists** and **Reincarnation,** deal primarily with spontaneous case reports and analyses. The seventh chapter, **Miscellaneous,** includes near-death experiences, out-of-body experiences, and articles of general interest. Some entries are listed more than once if they fall under two or more categories (e.g., under both **Clairvoyance** and **Precognition**).

These categories are meant more as guides than as gospel, and while the search was exhaustive, some articles may have been overlooked. We encourage the reader to let us know of any omissions or errors so that we may improve the bibliography for any future printings. For the reader needing some definitions of basic parapsychological terminology, a **Glossary** is included in Appendix A. Appendix B lists **Selected Parapsychology Research and Resource Centers.**

While compiling the bibliography, we encountered a lack of clearcut information about subject age in both titles and abstracts of articles. This made researching articles more arduous and may have led to unintentional omissions. For future reference, it would be helpful if researchers and editors kept in mind that relevant factors about subject populations and experiment types should be clear at a glance. Furthermore, not only in the area of children's ESP but in parapsychological literature in general, many valuable articles of use to researchers and others are unknown or buried. Bibliographies and overviews of research areas are of great help when readers are contemplating experiments or are reviewing the literature of parapsychology. We encourage others to consider undertaking similar bibliographies to add to the field's resources.

We have included six papers from a panel discussion, "Parapsychology and Children: 100 Years of Research," which we organized for the Thirty-Third Parapsychological Association Convention, Washington DC, August 1990. (The papers are abstracted in Research in Parapsychology 1990, convention proceedings, Scarecrow Press.)

The panelists were selected to give an overview of parapsychology and children in the areas of expertise related to the topic. The first three papers, on controversies, developmental issues, and classroom studies, deal primarily with the findings of laboratory research. The last three papers, two on the "exceptional human functions" children of China and one on past life memory (reincarnation) cases, deal primarily with spontaneous case material and how to evaluate it. An edited transcript of the discussion between panelists and audience members follows. We felt that including this material would offer the reader an overview of some of the continuing and contemporary issues involving parapsychological research with children.

PARAPSYCHOLOGY AND CHILDREN:

100 YEARS OF RESEARCH

Thirty-Third

Parapsychological Association

Convention

Washington, DC

August 17-20, 1990

CONTROVERSIES IN PARAPSYCHOLOGICAL RESEARCH WITH CHILDREN

Sally Ann Drucker, Ph.D.

Foundation for Research on the Nature of Man
Durham, NC

Since the 1880s, when Parapsychology began as a formal field of study, there have been numerous research articles, spontaneous case reports, and books on children's psi published. This panel was organized to give an overview of some of the findings on children's psi and to delineate some of the areas of controversy.

Controversy has surrounded parapsychology's work with children from the very beginning of the field. Young mediums, such as the Fox or Creery sisters, were caught in fraudulent acts. Some areas of spontaneous cases research, such as with poltergeists and past life memories, have focused primarily on children. In the papers that follow, Athena Drewes addresses developmental issues, including the macro-PK exhibited in poltergeist phenomena; the significance of age in past life memory cases is discussed by James G. Matlock. Current accusations of fraud, in relation to mini-Gellers and in particular the psychic children of China, are issues addressed by Drs. Krippner and Lee.

In turning to laboratory research, some of the most consistent results have been achieved in classroom studies. Dr. Kanthamani presents past and present findings, focusing on high school students. Also consistent is that certain factors, such as the sheep-goat effect and personality variables, appear to be the same for children as for adults. Nevertheless, several areas of laboratory research have had inconsistent results, such as the relationship of age to psi ability. The work of Spinelli on this subject, which seemed to indicate changes over an age range, was recently found to have statistical problems by Rick Berger (Berger, 1989). The M & M studies done by Athena Drewes and myself showed not age but IQ differences -- where high-IQ children did better on the second run, which seemed to indicate a learning effect (Drucker, Drewes, & Rubin, 1977). Other studies, however, have shown low-IQ children doing well on ESP tests (Bond, 1937; Shields, 1976). Since many children in western culture are in some sort of school setting even at ages three or four, eliminating the effect of education from consideration of age is hard to do. Although Giesler's studies in Brazil and Murray's in the Philippines did not confirm Winkelman's statistically significant results with children in Mexico (Giesler, 1985), more work with nonwestern children might be of use.

Trends in research with children, even theoretical explanations, have followed other cultural and research trends. For instance, in the 19th century, when children were perceived as more innocent and angelic than adults, they were also seen as closer to the spirit world and therefore more psychic. Then, post-Freud, children were perceived as less repressed than adults, or less angelic, and that was seen as a reason why they would be more psychic.

Perhaps the primary reason that children have been seen as ideal subjects, despite some difficulties of setting up experiments, is that children are assumed to be less affected by cultural norms than are adults. In 1937, Louisa E. Rhine put it this way: "It seemed likely that children, being more naive and less analytical than adults, might be particularly suitable as subjects for an investigation...results obtained from them are as free from bias as could be hoped for from any type of subject" (Rhine, 1937).

Currently, biological or psychoanalytic explanations may consist of children's greater use of right hemisphere processing or children's greater dependency predisposing them to rely on whatever sources of information are available. From the experimental evidence, however, it is not clear that children have greater ESP when younger than when older, although one study indicates that they have more ESP than adults do (Bottrill, 1969). Not enough work has been done to be able to make definitive statements. While it seems very plausible to assume that children should demonstrate high levels of psi, the research has not supported this conclusively. Experiments with both groups of children and individual children have shown significant psi, but no work with the general population except for Spinelli's, with its statistical problems, has shown psi at extraordinary levels.

Perhaps there are several questions that we need to ask:

1) If we test the same child or children over a period of time, how do we separate changes over an age span from what might be a possible decline effect? If we keep testing, when do changes actually relate to age and when do they relate to boredom?

2) If the same experiment is done with different ages of children, is it appropriate for both the younger and older children? If

not, then it does not tell us if age affects psi, since the scoring difference might be due to the appropriateness or inappropriateness of the experiment.

3) Jan Ehrenwald presented the concept of a psi filter that is perhaps more permeable for children. Yet if this filter is there for reasons of biological survival, screening out noise, trivia, and unpleasantness, why would anyone, especially a child, want to drop it in a situation where he or she does not feel totally safe? How safe does a child feel in an experimental laboratory situation with an unknown adult? Even, or especially, in a classroom situation, how safe is it for a child to drop that screen? Perhaps the fact that experimental results with children have been as good as they have been, despite the insecurity and inappropriateness of many experimental situations, speaks to the idea that children do indeed possess special abilities after all.

Dr. Kanthamani and I independently came to the conclusion that a meta-analysis of the school studies might be of use and could tell us more about the psi level of children as a group than individual studies could. We encourage further work in this area.

REFERENCES

Berger, R. E. (1989). A critical examination of the Spinelli dissertation data. Journal of the Society for Psychical Research, 56, 28-34.

Bond, E. M. (1937). General extrasensory perception with a group of fourth and fifth grade children. Journal of Parapsychology, 1, 114-122.

Bottrill, J. (1969). Effects of motivation on ESP. Journal of Parapsychology, 33, 70.

Drucker, S. A., Drewes, A. A., & Rubin, L. (1977). ESP in relation to cognitive development and IQ in young children. Journal of the American Society for Psychical Research, 71, 289-298.

Ehrenwald, J. (1948). Telepathy and Medical Psychology NY: W. W. Norton & Co., 198.

Giesler, P. V. (1985). An attempted replication of Winkelman's ESP and socialization research [Summary]. In R. A. White & J. Solfvin (Eds.), Research in Parapsychology 1984 (pp. 24-27). Metuchen, NJ: Scarecrow Press.

Murray, D. M. (1983). The effect of schooling on the manifestation of clairvoyant abilities among Isnag children of the Northern Philippines [Summary]. In W. G. Roll, J. Beloff, & R. A. White (Eds.), Research in Parapsychology 1982 (pp. 245-248). Metuchen, NJ: Scarecrow Press.

Rhine, L. E. (1937). Some stimulus variations in extra-sensory perception with child subjects. Journal of Parapsychology, 1, 102-113.

Shields, E. (1976). Severely mentally retarded children's psi ability [Summary]. In J. D. Morris, W. G. Roll, & R. L. Morris (Eds.), Research in Parapsychology 1975 (p. 139). Metuchen, NJ: Scarecrow Press.

Spinelli, E. (1977). The effects of chronological age on GESP ability [Summary]. In J. D. Morris, W. G. Roll, & R. L. Morris (Eds.), Research in Parapsychology 1976 (pp. 122-124). Metuchen, NJ: Scarecrow Press.

Winkelman, M. (1981). The effects of schooling and formal education upon extrasensory abilities [Summary]. In W. G. Roll & J. Beloff (Eds.), Research in Parapsychology 1980 (pp. 26-29). Metuchen, NJ: Scarecrow Press.

CHILDREN'S DEVELOPMENT AND ESP

Athena A. Drewes, M.A., M.S., Psy.D. Candidate

Pace University
New York, NY

Louisa Rhine (1968) wrote in Hidden Channels of the Mind that "the interesting general fact that emerges from studying children is that their experiences, though simpler, still are similar both in form and type to those of adults. It seems that ESP may be 'there' even in childhood." Parapsychologists have sought to explore whether ESP has a developmental component, the types of psi phenomena children manifest, whether psi phenomena diminishes with age, and the earliest age that psi can be tested and demonstrated.

FitzHerbert (1960) proposed that telepathy occurrences between mother and child go as far back as prenatal and even pre-embryonic memories. Children are particularly responsive to the unconscious feelings of others (especially their mothers'). Tauber and Green (1959) raised the question of whether the use of prelogical faculties for ESP is a regression to an infantile state. Ehrenwald (1971) theorized that "telepathy is the embryological matrix of communication which is later destined to be suppressed by speech. It may be a vitally important means of communication serving the integration and smooth functioning of the mother-child unit and thereby its very survival as a viable entity."

Because of the natural dependency stage of the child, a symbiotic relationship from prebirth through around two years of age develops between child and mother. This intense closeness sets the stage for the occurrence of psychic phenomena. Mothers report that, around this age, telepathic events occur in relation to their saving their child from some disaster or event that is about to happen. As the child progresses developmentally, various shifts in the types of psi phenomena may occur.

Ehrenwald (1972) further postulated that psi phenomena become repressed and substituted for by "normal" perceptual and motoric processes through development. Telepathy and clairvoyance would be extensions of normal perceptual processes: precognition as the reverse of retrospective memory and PK as an extension of motoric abilities. Psi states show characteristics of Freud's primary-process functioning, of symbolic representation, of prelogic or of Piaget's preoperational thinking. Spinelli (1987), in his controversial research, suggested that children who are in the early stages of conscious self-development will manifest greater GESP. Once a stable, conscious self-identity has been formed, GESP will be greatly reduced.

Research has attempted to look at these issues. Children, (ages 6 weeks to late teens) have been subjects. Braud (1981) tested infants (ages 6 weeks to 12 months) for time-displaced PK, using the playback of their mothers' voices as feedback. Bierman (1983) used 10-month-old infants in testing for PK abilities with micro-computers. Results of these tests were varied. Stevenson (1983) found Indian children began speaking about past life memories at 38 months, with those memories fading around 79 months. Children's near death experiences are reported as similar both in content and sequence to those of adults. School-age children have been tested extensively by Anderson, White, Freeman, and Van Busschbach, among others. They have found evidence of psi across all ages and types of tests. Shargal (1987) recently found that first graders scored better than fourth-grade children on clairvoyance tasks. Winkelman (1981) tested Mexican children (ages 8-14) on clairvoyance, PK, and precognition tasks. He found clairvoyance and precognition scores correlated negatively with math ability, years of schooling, and age. PK scores correlated positively with age. However, Giesler (1985) failed to replicate this study using children in Brazil. Nvomeysky (1984) reviewed a series of color telepathy experiments in the USSR. Studies showed adolescents (ages 14-15) have a better capacity for color telepathy and that color telepathy decreases with age. Roll has reported extensively on Recurrent Spontaneous Psychokinesis (RSPK) occurring predominantly with adolescents. Repressed or unconscious hostilities are often directed through RSPK events. Children of all ages have reported spontaneous PK, telepathic, clairvoyant, and precognitive experiences.

Child personality factors seem to follow the same general trend as those of adults. Shields (1962) found that withdrawn children have significantly lower ESP scores than nonwithdrawn children. Kanthamani and Rao (1972) found that high schoolers who were assertive, extroverted, expansive, and low on neuroticism scored significantly higher on ESP tasks. Tension and anxiety can lower ESP scores. Children of school age have already become test conscious and often regard the ESP task as a test. IQ has also been shown to have varying results in relation to ESP. Drucker, Drewes, & Rubin (1977) found children with a high IQ seemed to accomplish learning better with immediate feedback during an ESP task. Even children's belief in ESP and their relationship with agents or experimenters can significantly impact on children's ESP scores, as it does for adults.

In conclusion, the research seems to confirm Louisa Rhine's statement. Children's ESP experiences are similar both in type and form to those of adults with the addition of developmental considerations. But unlike adult studies, children have been under-utilized as laboratory subjects. There has been a large body of work collected on past life memories, RSPK phenomena, and teenage personality characteristics. However, lab research has not been systematic in exploring and replicating studies dealing with the issue of development. It has lacked longitudinal studies and cluster studies, such as are done with adult Ganzfeld and Remote Viewing experiments, to help conclusively settle the issue of development and ESP. Future work needs to be done in this area.

REFERENCES

Bierman, D. J. (1983). Exploring the fundamental hypothesis of the observational theories using a PK test for babies. [Summary]. In W. G. Roll, J. Beloff, & R. A. White (Eds.), Research in Parapsychology 1982 (p. 97). Metuchen, NJ: Scarecrow Press.

Braud, W. (1981). Psychokinesis experiments with infants and young children. [Summary]. In W. G. Roll & J. Beloff (Eds.), Research in Parapsychology 1980 (pp. 30-31). Metuchen, NJ: Scarecrow Press.

Drucker, S. A., Drewes, A. A., & Rubin, L. (1977). ESP in relation to cognitive development in young children. Journal of the American Society for Psychical Research, 71, 289-298.

Ehrenwald, J. (1971). Mother-child symbiosis: Cradle of ESP. Psychoanalytic Review, 58, 455-466.

Ehrenwald, J. (1972). A neurophysiological model of psi phenomena. Journal of Nervous and Mental Disease, 154, 406-418.

FitzHerbert, J. (1960). Role of extrasensory perception in early childhood. Journal of Mental Science, 106, 1560-1567.

Giesler, P. V. (1985). An attempted replication of Winkelman's ESP and socialization research. [Summary]. In R. A. White & J. Solfvin (Eds.). Research in Parapsychology 1984 (pp. 24-27). Metuchen, NJ: Scarecrow Press.

Kanthamani, B. K. & Rao, K. R. (1971). Personality characteristics of ESP subjects: I. Primary personality characteristics and ESP. Journal of Parapsychology 35, 189-207.

Nvomeysky, A. (1984). On the possible effect of an experimenter's subliminal or telepathic influence on dermo-optic sensitivity. PSI Research 3, 8-15.

Rhine, L. E. (1968). Hidden Channels of the Mind. NY: William Sloane, 148-160.

Shargal, S. (1987). Children's ESP scores in relation to age [Summary]. In D. H. Weiner & R. D. Nelson (Eds.). Research in Parapsychology 1986 (pp. 51-53). Metuchen, NJ: Scarecrow Press.

Shields, E. (1962). Comparison of children's guessing ability with personality characteristics. Journal of Parapsychology, 26, 200-210.

Spinelli, E. (1987). Child development and GESP: A summary. Parapsychology Review, 18, 8-11.

Stevenson, I. (1983). American children who claim to remember previous lives. Journal of Nervous and Mental Disease, 171, 742-748.

Tauber, E. S. & Green, M. (1959). Prelogical experience. NY: Basic Books.

Winkelman, M. (1981). The effect of formal education on extra-sensory abilities: The Ozolco study. Journal of Parapsychology, 45, 321-336.

PSI ABILITY AMONG YOUTH

H. Kanthamani, Ph.D.

Foundation for Research on the Nature of Man
Durham, NC

A huge portion of research in parapsychology over the years has utilized young people, who are mostly high school and college students, as subjects. Did the researchers seek the participation of such youngsters assuming that they would demonstrate greater psi ability than other possible subjects? Although there is some theoretical justification to expect that people probably are more "psi-prone" when younger than when older, I doubt if this was the driving force for the numerous investigators who have worked with young people all through the history of parapsychology. On the other hand, factors such as ready availability, and the enthusiastic cooperation normally shown by the young volunteers, have attracted more and more research projects focused on such populations. Rarely, however, is any evaluation of the effectiveness of a given project assessed merely by the standpoint of subject population. It is likely that such project reviews would more often reflect a host of factors that contribute to the success in the test, while being young or old could just be one factor. It is not in the scope of the present paper to attempt a comprehensive review. The purpose here is only to briefly point out the general lines of research contributed by work with youth, and even here, I am restricting myself to the high school population.

Classroom studies form a major milestone in the history of experimental parapsychology. Although as early as 1937 E. M. Bond tested grade school children for ESP (Bond, 1937), it was only in the 1950s that the notion of utilizing a classroom situation for actual testing purposes began. Van Busschbach (1953) conducted a series of ESP tests with grade school children using a GESP task. He obtained highly significant results with primary school children when the teacher was the sender. The results, however, were not significant with the secondary school students. Further, when a stranger or fellow student took the role of sender, the significance level dropped considerably. These findings led to the idea that the rapport is strongest between teachers and students, and this is something that need not be created just for the ESP testing, but that exists naturally. It is possible to assume that this rapport is much stronger with young children than older ones, which may be responsible for the different results obtained with them. A classroom setting with an active role for the teacher formed the model for further work both in Holland and other countries.

Many replication attempts followed after the original Van Busschbach study. His own work (1955, 1959) continued to provide further evidence of strong results with primary school children in Holland; however, with American schools (1956) it was not so well marked. Van Busschbach noted that the key ingredient, namely the mutual rapport between teachers and students, did not seem as high in American schools as compared to the Dutch schools.

Many years later, Randall (1972) attempted another cross-cultural replication in England with grammar school students. He used the same paradigm as Van Busschbach, having the teacher as the sender, and tested a number of groups. Unfortunately, the results showed no evidence of psi in the data. On the other hand, Bierman and Camstra (1973) obtained highly successful results with Dutch primary and secondary school children. Thus, there appear to be strong cultural differences, as noted by Van Busschbach himself, in the atmosphere of the classrooms from one country to another. While the teacher-pupil interaction is presumably present in all classroom situations, it is probably their attitude toward each other that is different from one society to another. While we are quite familiar with the role of the sheep-goat effect in parapsychology, the classroom studies provide a unique opportunity to test if the mutual rapport between teacher and students would affect the psi performance. It is in this area that Anderson and White made a remarkable contribution.

In a long series of experiments, Anderson and White (1956) attempted replicating Van Busschbach's model in working with high school students, by having their teachers administer the ESP tests. Although there was no overall significance in these data, a strong interaction occurred with the attitude variable relating to the mutual like-dislike between the teachers and pupils. They elicited students' attitudes toward teachers and teachers' attitudes toward the students. Those with a mutually positive attitude showed above-chance scores, while others with negative attitude obtained below-chance scores. The difference between the two groups was highly significant.

In these studies, Anderson and White selected teachers to act as the test administrators and to carry out the ESP test in a class of their choice. Instead of the GESP mode used by Van Busschbach, they adopted a clairvoyance method. Anderson and White made a significant methodological improvement by developing a procedure for group testing, using individualized target sets for each subject. By using random number tables, each target sheet was prepared with the required number of runs and sealed in an envelope. A response sheet was attached to the outside of the envelope, on which the subject wrote his or her responses. This was the beginning of the more popularly known "envelope clairvoyance method," which is commonly used even today.

Several attempts at replication (Anderson & White, 1957, 1958c) were equally successful, which added to the overall robustness of the Anderson-White findings. They tried to extend this to include lower-grade children, with similar results (Anderson, 1957). In another study (1958b) they compared the test results administered in the beginning of the semester to those obtained from a second testing done at the end of the semester. Their findings suggested that the teacher-pupil attitudes tend to get stronger over a period of time, and therefore, one should expect better results when ESP tests are conducted at the end of the school term. Another extension of the Anderson-White technique included testing the relationship between ESP scores and the grade levels of the students (Anderson, 1959). As can be expected, the two showed a positive relationship. Further, the mutual attitudes of the teacher and pupils interacted with the students' grade levels. These findings should be interesting for parapsychologists and in the field of educational psychology as well.

While the above studies involved a clairvoyance strategy, Anderson and White (1958a) conducted a study using a GESP procedure. They had two teachers acting as senders, who sent different target sequences, unknown to the students. While the results were similar, as before, it was independently significant for only one teacher, which suggested individual differences among the teachers as another variable.

In 1960s and 70s, the parapsychology scene was swamped by a number of investigators who used both group testing methods and individual testing methods with high school and junior high school students. One line of research was carried out by John Freeman and Winnifred Nielsen in correlating ESP scores with anxiety scores obtained by the Manifest Anxiety Scale (MAS). In a long series of experiments, they found that high-anxious subjects scored higher than low-anxious, while the mid-anxious scored the lowest (Freeman & Nielsen, 1964; Nielsen & Freeman, 1965). K. R. Rao (1965), on the other hand, found a negative correlation with MAS scores and ESP scores. The contradiction between these two studies was attributed to the type of ESP task used by them. The language ESP test used by

Rao was regarded as complex, while the precognition test of Freeman and Nielsen was considered as simple. Honorton (1967) manipulated subjects' expectancy of the difficulty level of the ESP task and found interesting results according to his expectation. It is interesting to note that these studies were carried out in the same lab at about the same time period, and with some of the same subjects, yet the results were quite varied. Findings like these contributed to the growing emphasis on the role of experimenters in psi research.

Another line of research at this time was initiated by Martin Johnson (Carpenter, 1965; Johnson & Kanthamani, 1967), who used a projective test known as the Defense Mechanism Test (DMT) to correlate with ESP scores. In general, the studies showed a negative correlation, which suggested low defensiveness as an indicator of psi hitting. This line of work was continued later by Erlendur Haraldsson (Johnson & Haraldsson, 1984) in Iceland, with both high school and college students. Haraldsson, et al., in a meta-analysis, showed that the DMT predictions were highly significant over the different studies done until then (Haraldsson, Houtkooper, & Hoeltje, 1987).

ESP testing using words in two languages formed another major line of research started by K. R. Rao in the 1960s. He used five words in English and their equivalents in Telugu (an Indian language) as the targets and tested a large number of students, both high school and college. In general, subjects scored positively on Telugu targets and missed on English, with a significant difference between the two (Rao, 1963, 1964, 1979). This pattern, however, was later found to interact with the sex of the subjects and the experimenters, and their familiarity and identification with the languages used (Rao & Davis, 1978). The language-ESP tests, therefore, can be regarded as a sensitive indicator of interpersonal variables.

Junior high school students have also made a mark on the parapsychology scene, as can be seen from the following studies. In one study, Carpenter (1971) found an interesting interaction between the anxiety scores (obtained from the MAS) of the subjects and the type of target (neutral or emotional) in determining their ESP scores. In another study, Kanthamani (1966) tested pairs of kids in a competitive situation and obtained strong differences between the "expected hitters" and "expected missers." She felt that if competition is a psi-conducive variable, it should be strong among the adolescent children.

Personality studies were another main line of research done with young people. Kanthamani and Rao (1971), in an attempt to explore the personality aspects of the ESP subjects, carried out an elaborate study in India, selecting 16- to 18-year-olds from high school and junior college. They used Cattell's High School Personality Questionnaire (HSPQ), along with ESP tests. In a series of four experiments, Kanthamani and Rao (1972, 1973a) found that warm, sociable, self-assured, and easy-going subjects obtained psi-hitting, while their counterparts, characterized as being aloof, critical, insecure, and uptight, produced psi-missing. When a graphic expansive-compressive measure was used on these subjects, an interesting interaction with the extraversion scores was noticed in predicting the subjects' ESP performance (Kanthamani & Rao, 1973b).

The above line of research was later continued at FRNM in the late 1970s by Kanthamani, JoMarie Haight, and Jim Kennedy, when they planned an extended project involving a number of variables. This was an attempt at collecting systematic data from a large number of subjects from the high school population. As it happened, we continued the project for about four years and collected a massive amount of data representing over 500 subjects, which has not been analyzed as yet. Only a small portion relating to the spontaneous experiences has been reported earlier (Haight 1979), which is very interesting. In this, the investigators noted that some subjects, although a small percentage of the subject pool, reported experiences that could be considered as genuine forms of psi. The form and type of these experiences appeared to be similar to the larger collection of L. E. Rhine. The personality interactions of these subjects showed that, while there were no differences on the well-known personality factors between those reporting an experience and those who did not, there were wide differences between the two groups on attitude variables (Kanthamani, Haight, & Kennedy, 1979). While these findings are interesting by themselves, this area could definitely be further explored, as spontaneous experiences do occur among young people.

Many other studies have attempted to correlate certain cognitive variables with ESP scores. The memory area has been of great interest to many. Just to mention a few: Sally Feather (1967) reported a positive correlation between ESP scores and memory scores of her subjects. Using a paired-associate learning strategy, Kanthamani and Rao (1974) found that within each subject the correctly recalled trials were associated with psi-hitting, while the incorrectly recalled trials showed psi-missing. K. R. Rao developed yet another form of testing memory and ESP and has reported many studies with interesting results (Rao, Morrison, & Davis, 1977; Rao, Morrison, Davis, & Freeman, 1977).

Other areas of research included the following: inducing response biases in subjects to see their influence on ESP scoring

(Kanthamani & Rao, 1975); creating different attentional sets (passive and active) in relation to ESP scoring (Kanthamani, 1985); target characteristics, namely, imagery, concreteness, and meaning and psi (Kanthamani & Rao, 1979, 1980; Morrison, 1979); psi in relation to volition (Rao, Kanthamani, & Krishna, 1979); speculating that personality tests (mood check lists) themselves could form nonintentional psi tasks (Kennedy & Haight, 1977); and finally, attempted replication of Anderson & White technique (Haight & Weiner, 1981).

The above review necessarily is a cursory one, and it is hoped it will stimulate a much broader review using more sophisticated procedures. Also, this might lead to more systematic research to utilize the abundant "youth power" that we have around us.

REFERENCES

Anderson, M. & White, R. (1956). Teacher-pupil attitudes and clairvoyance test results. Journal of Parapsychology, 20, 141-157.

Anderson, M. (1957). Clairvoyance and teacher-pupil attitudes in fifth and sixth grades. Journal of Parapsychology, 21, 1-12.

Anderson, M. (1959). The relationship between level of ESP scoring and student class grade. Journal of Parapsychology, 23, 1-18.

Anderson, M. & White, R. (1957). A further investigation of teacher-pupil attitudes and clairvoyance test results. Journal of Parapsychology, 21, 81-97.

Anderson, M. & White, R. (1958a). ESP score level in relation to students' attitude toward teacher-agents acting simultaneously. Journal of Parapsychology, 22, 20-28.

Anderson, M. & White, R. (1958b). The relationship between changes in student attitude and ESP scoring. Journal of Parapsychology, 22, 167-174.

Anderson, M. & White, R. (1958c). A survey of work on ESP and teacher-pupil attitudes. Journal of Parapsychology, 22, 246-268.

Bierman, D. J. & Camstra, B. (1973). GESP in the classroom. [Summary]. In W. G. Roll, R. L. Morris, & J. D. Morris (Eds.), Research in Parapsychology 1972 (pp. 168-170). Metuchen, NJ: Scarecrow Press.

Bond, E. M. (1937). General extrasensory perception with a group of fourth and fifth grade retarded children. Journal of Parapsychology, 2, 123-142.

Carpenter, J. C. (1965). An exploratory test of ESP in relation to anxiety proneness. In J. B. Rhine & Associates (Eds.), Parapsychology: From Duke to FRNM (pp. 68-73). Durham, NC: Parapsychology Press.

Carpenter, J. C. (1971). The differential effect and hidden target differences consisting of erotic and neutral stimuli. Journal of the American Society for Psychical Research, 65, 204-214.

Feather, S. R. (1967). A quantitative comparison of memory and ESP. Journal of Parapsychology, 31, 93-98.

Freeman, J. A. & Nielsen, W. (1964). Precognition score deviations as related to anxiety levels. Journal of Parapsychology, 28, 239-249.

Haight, J. M. (1979). Spontaneous psi cases: A survey and preliminary study of ESP, attitudes, and personality relationships. Journal of Parapsychology, 43, 179-204.

Haight, J. M., Kanthamani, H., & Kennedy, J. E. (1978). A study of spontaneous experiences among unselected high-school students. Journal of Parapsychology, 42, 67-68.

Haight, J. M., Kanthamani, H., & Kennedy, J. E. (1979). Further work on spontaneous cases from high-school students. Journal of Parapsychology, 43, 53-54.

Haight, J. M., Kennedy, J. E., & Kanthamani, H. (1979). Spontaneous psi experiences among unselected high school subjects [Summary]. In W. G. Roll (Ed.), Research in Parapsychology 1978 (pp. 46-47). Metuchen, NJ: Scarecrow Press.

Haight, J. & Weiner, D. H. (1981). A new inquiry into the effect of teacher-pupil attitude on clairvoyance performance. Journal of Parapsychology, 45, 154-155.

Haraldsson, E., Houtkooper, J. M., & Hoeltje, C. (1987). The Defense Mechanism Test as a predictor of ESP performance: Icelandic study VII and meta-analysis of thirteen experiments. Journal of Parapsychology, 51, 75-90.

Honorton, C. (1967). The relationship between ESP and manifest anxiety level. Journal of Parapsychology, 29, 291-292.

Johnson, M. & Kanthamani, B. K. (1967). The Defense Mechanism Test as a predictor of ESP scoring direction. Journal of Parapsychology, 31, 99-110.

Johnson, M. & Haraldsson, E. (1984). The Defense Mechanism Test as a predictor of ESP scores: Icelandic studies IV and V. Journal of Parapsychology, 48, 185-200.

Kanthamani, B. K. (1966). ESP and social stimulus. Journal of Parapsychology, 30, 31-38.

Kanthamani, B. K. & Rao, K. R. (1971). Personality characteristics of ESP subjects: I. Primary personality characteristics and ESP. Journal of Parapsychology, 35, 189-207.

Kanthamani, B. K. & Rao, K. R. (1972). Personality characteristics of ESP subjects: III. Extraversion and ESP. Journal of Parapsychology, 36, 198-212.

Kanthamani, B. K. & Rao, K. R. (1973a). Personality characteristics of ESP subjects: IV. Neuroticism and ESP. Journal of Parapsychology, 37, 37-50.

Kanthamani, B. K. & Rao, K. R. (1973b). Personality characteristics of ESP subjects: V. Graphic expansiveness and ESP. Journal of Parapsychology, 37, 119-129.

Kanthamani, H. (1985). Attentional sets and ESP scores [Summary]. In R. A. White & J. Solfvin (Eds.), Research in Parapsychology 1984 (pp. 82-85). Metuchen, NJ: Scarecrow Press.

Kanthamani, H., Haight, J., & Kennedy, J. E. (1979). Personality and spontaneous experiences: An exploratory study [Summary]. In W. G. Roll (Ed.), Research in Parapsychology 1978 (pp. 47-49). Metuchen, NJ: Scarecrow Press.

Kanthamani, H. & Rao, H. H. (1974). A study of memory-ESP relationships using linguistic forms. Journal of Parapsychology, 38, 286-300.

Kanthamani, H. & Rao, H. H. (1975). Response tendencies and stimulus structure, Journal of Parapsychology, 39, 97-105.

Kanthamani, H. & Rao, K. R. (1979). Imagery, concreteness, and meaningfulness of target words in relation to psi-scoring: A preliminary experiment. Journal of Parapsychology, 43, 46-47.

Kanthamani, H. & Rao, K. R. (1980). Psi scoring in relation to imagery, concreteness, and meaningfulness attributes of target words. Journal of Parapsychology, 44, 79-80.

Kennedy, J. E. & Haight, J. (1977). Psychological tests as nonintentional psi tasks: A vehicle for experimenter effects. Journal of Parapsychology, 41, 48-49.

Morrison, M. D. (1979). Examining the role of imagery in psi. Journal of Parapsychology, 43, 47-48.

Nielsen, W. & Freeman, J. A. (1965). Consistency of relationships between ESP and emotional variables. Journal of Parapsychology, 29, 75-88.

Randall, J. (1972). Group experiments with schoolboys. Journal of Parapsychology, 36, 133-143.

Rao, K. R. (1963). Studies in the preferential effect: II. A language ESP test involving precognition and intervention. Journal of Parapsychology, 27, 147-160.

Rao, K. R. (1964). The role of key cards in preferential response situations. Journal of Parapsychology, 28, 23-41.

Rao, K. R. (1965). ESP and the manifest anxiety scale. Journal of Parapsychology, 29, 12-18.

Rao, K. R. (1979). ESP tests under normal and relaxed conditions. Journal of Parapsychology, 43, 1-16.

Rao, K. R. & Davis, J. W. (1978). The differential effect and experimenter effects in intentional and nonintentional psi tests. Journal of Parapsychology, 42, 1-17.

Rao, K. R., Kanthamani, H., & Krishna, S. R. (1979). Psi and volitional activity: An experimental study of psi in a competitive situation. Journal of Parapsychology, 43, 101-112.

Rao, K. R., Morrison, M., & Davis, J. W. (1977). Paired-associates recall and ESP: A study of memory and psi-missing. Journal of Parapsychology, 41, 165-189.

Rao, K. R., Morrison, M., Davis, J. W., & Freeman, J. A. (1977). The role of association in memory-recall and ESP. Journal of Parapsychology, 41, 190-197.

Van Busschbach, J. G. (1953). An investigation of extrasensory perception in school children. Journal of Parapsychology, 17, 210-214.

Van Busschbach, J. G. (1955). A further report on an investigation of ESP in school children. Journal of Parapsychology, 19, 73-81.

Van Busschbach, J. G. (1956). An investigation of ESP between teachers and pupils in American schools. Journal of Parapsychology, 20, 71-80.

Van Busschbach, J. G. (1959). An investigation of ESP in the first and second grades of Dutch schools. Journal of Parapsychology, 23, 227-237.

THE EXCEPTIONAL HUMAN FUNCTIONS RESEARCH IN CHINA

Raymond Lee, Ph.D.

San Diego State University
San Diego, CA

In November 1989, I was invited to deliver a speech at the Second National Conference on Somatic Science in Beijing, where several hundred professors, scientists, researchers, and psychics from various parts of the People's Republic of China gathered to share research results and new ideas. Thanks to the arrangements of professor Shu-Huang Lin, Director of the Comprehensive Technology Institute, Beijing Teachers College, while I was in Beijing we conducted five research projects together. In this paper, I report on paranormal phenomena demonstrated by two psychics who were discovered in the late 1970s and early 1980s when they were young; they still claim to possess exceptional functions of the human body (EHF).

Our first investigation was conducted in an unheated hotel room during the middle of the convention. The EHF woman, from Wuhan City (in the central part of China), was supposedly, since she was a child, mentally able to identify messages from sealed envelopes, bend metal spoons, and remove pills from sealed bottles.

Unfortunately, the testing conditions were poor and chaotic. The room was cold, noisy, and packed with curious and unnecessary observers. Her physical and psychological states were not optimal either. She was tired, sick, and nervous when contacted by us to see if she was willing to be tested. Nevertheless, she was eager to try and take the sealed envelope that I had prepared and brought from the United States. She attempted to identify the written Chinese character sealed in it. Her attempt was not successful.

Next, she tried to remove the pills from a presealed glass made by a professional glass blower in San Diego. This attempt was also unsuccessful. Finally, she tried to bend mentally my tiny stainless steel suitcase key. She put it in her palms, placed both hands in front of her face, closed her eyes and then quietly meditated for two to three minutes. When she opened her palms, it was bent. It is extremely difficult, if not impossible, even for a strong man to bend a tiny stainless steel key between two palms under close observation. Since I was sitting only two feet from her, and my video camera was continuously monitering her actions, the possibility of trickery was low.

After the experiment, she apologized for not being able to demonstrate successfully her other psychic abilities. She invited me to come to Wuhan to visit her school and have a longer stay, so that she could retry the experiments under optimal conditions. Unfortunately, due to a tight schedule, I was not able to accept that offer.

The second experiment was conducted with one of the most famous psychics in China, Mr. Pao Hsien Chang. Unfortunately, he declined most of the experimental protocols that I had brought from the United States. He did, however, conduct several demonstrations.

The first was to use his finger to burn a heavy jacket. A common magician can also do this, therefore making it impossible to distinguish if it is a genuine psychic power. After the experiment, he touched my leg with his finger, giving me a strong and painful electric shock. He claimed that his finger carried electric current. He also took and blew on my camera; the film was automatically rewound! He then threatened to destroy my video camera if I wanted to prove his psychic powers. Since I did not want to take the chance of losing this important piece of scientific monitoring equipment during my stay in Beijing, I begged him not to do this trick. During lunch, to show his powers, with his left hand he grasped a heavy duty silver spoon (with a long and strong handle) from the table, blew on it, and used his right hand to twist the handle of the spoon quickly and effortlessly a couple of times. When he opened his left hand, the handle of the spoon was still kept upright but twisted around at least five times. The whole process took less than five seconds. When I touched the spoon right after the demonstration, it remained cold.

For the second demonstration, Mr. Chang attempted to remove the pills from the unopened bottle that Professor Lin had bought from a Beijing drug store. Before the experiment, it was examined to make sure that none of the two seals were broken: an inner cork sealed with wax, and an outer metal cap on top of the bottle. Several people, including myself, sat around him within two to ten feet, making it extremely difficult for him to cheat. Mr. Chang grasped the bottle in his left hand and asked me to put my palm under it. He then proceeded to shake the bottle. Within five seconds, two-thirds of the 100 pills were dropping from the bottom of the bottle to my hand.

Since we did not mark the bottle, I am not completely sure that the claimed powers were authentic. When I asked why Mr. Chang declined to try my presealed glass that I had brought from the United States, Professor Lin told me that every new glass or material is a challenge. Mr. Chang needs to take hours or even days and try many times before he can perform any new task. Since Mr. Chang is not a scientist and did not even graduate from an elementary school, it is very difficult for him to understand and accept the rigorous requirements of a scientific experiment. The responsibility of a researcher is to design an experiment that is preplanned, rigorous, and yet well suited to the psychic person (Krippner, 1990). A researcher, like a child psychologist, must have the patience to wait hours, days, weeks, or even months to gain the trust and cooperation of the psychic, in order to capture the necessary results. Sometimes psychics, like children, may cheat to maintain face. It is our responsibility, as scientific researchers, to distinguish between authentic and spurious paranormal powers.

Professor Lin showed me several videotapes of more rigorous studies and other research papers (Zhu & Zhu, 1989) which indicate that Mr. Chang and other persons with that particular EHF ability, after hours of effort, might be able to move pills and even bugs from the professionally made presealed glasses. (The only other way to remove the objects would be to break the glass).

For the next demonstration, he asked me to go to the corner of the room, secretly write a Chinese character on a piece of paper, fold it, and put it on the edge of the coffee table near him. He used the tip of his forefinger to touch the crumpled paper ball twice and picked it up with two fingers. In three seconds, he correctly identified the Chinese character. Amazingly, he also told me that my handwriting was not clear, which was correct because my pen was dry and I could not write clearly.

Next, he picked up the same pill bottle used before, turned it upside down, took the crumpled paper ball with two fingers, and pushed it against the bottom of the bottle. We saw the paper ball disappear and emerge into the bottle. The whole process took less than five seconds. I opened the metal cap and examined the inner wax sealed cork; it was not broken. I decided not to open the inner cork right away to verify that my handwritten paper ball was indeed inside that bottle. I brought the bottle back to the United

States and examined it in front of Professor Long Chi Lee, an internationally known physics professor at San Diego State University. Indeed, the paper ball was inside that bottle. To correctly identify the Chinese character simply by touching the paper ball twice, and put it inside a double-sealed bottle within five seconds, strongly indicates that EHF may really exist.

The final demonstration is even more shocking. In the United States, I had printed beforehand a unique business card with my Chinese name and a fake address and telephone number. The fake parts were to assure that it was a one-and-only original that could not be duplicated. Mr. Chang picked up the card and asked a Japanese professor to sign a Chinese character on it. He then folded the card several times and asked another person to chew it until it was totally destroyed. Mr. Chang asked that person to spit out the remains and put them in his palms. He started to rub the destroyed card. I was sitting only two feet from him; therefore, I could see the procedure very clearly. First, I saw a business card that had been broken into half a dozen pieces in his palms. Then, he blew on them and the pieces became a whole card again with no printing on it. He blew on the blank card one more time and showed me that all the printing except the Japanese professor's signature had reappeared. He proceeded to blow on the card one more time. When he returned the card to me, the signature, in addition to the printing, reappeared.

To check if this was really a display of authentic psychic powers, I examined all possibilities. Mr. Chang could have hidden the original and given another card to be destroyed. If this were true, he would merely have to reveal the original that had not even been folded and chewed in the first place. Since I forgot to tear up the card personally before he asked someone to chew it, this could have been the case. However, there are three pieces of evidence against this possibility:

1) I compared it with an identical textured card (with different printing) that I had brought along. The fiber texture of the card was slightly different from before, probably from the saliva. This indicates that the original was indeed chewed up.

2) Mr. Chang had folded it several times before the destroying process. The "repaired" card had a small trace of one crease. If he did not fold the original in the first place, the trace of crease should not have been there.

3) A second folding line appeared two days later. This indicates that the repairing process was not finished. Also, this indicates that the card was indeed folded at least twice before.

Otherwise, the second trace of crease would not reappear two days later. If he did hide the original, why was there no trace of the second folding line immediately after the experiment?

Another possibility was that Mr. Chang could have destroyed the original and replaced it with a totally different card. Again, this is not likely, because as I have already mentioned, the card was completely unique.

Finally, Professor Lin told me that they had conducted similar studies with Mr. Chang and other psychics before. In those cases, they did tear up the card personally. Mr. Chang and other persons with this particular ability still were able to repair the original. It is also interesting to note that upon request, Mr. Chang was able to change the order of the words on the card during the repairing process. If all this can be proven to be true, the implications of this psychic power will be scientifically significant.

In addition, Professor Wang (1989), from a western medical school in northeastern China, presented a research paper at the convention which showed that a female medical student had the psychic power to repair broken leaves. The repairing process lasted twenty-three minutes to four hours. However, the broken traces could still be seen under microscopic observation. The experiment has been successfully replicated three times, at different locations, under rigorous conditions.

In conclusion, since the procedures we have used in these studies were not conducted under ideal standards, the exceptional human functions cannot be conclusively proven. Nevertheless, there is a strong possibility that EHF does exist. The stakes are high. Apparently, more rigorous and well-controlled laboratory studies are urgently needed. If the same results appear under better testing conditions, it would also be worth investigating the special training techniques used with children who demonstrate EHF.

REFERENCES

Krippner, S. (1990). A display of powers: Peeking at China's psychic children. Paper presented at the 33rd Annual PA Convention, Washington, DC. In extended form in this volume as Observing Psychic Wonderkids: Pitfalls and Precautions.

Wang, C. Y., Sou, Z. M., & Pu, H. K. (1989). A laboratory study on the psychic powers of repairing broken leaves. Paper presented at the Second National Conference of Somatic Science, Beijing, China.

Zhu, R. L. & Zhu, Y. (1989). Chuang Jian Ren Ti Ke Xue Sichuan, China: Sichuan Educational Publishing Co., 647-717.

OBSERVING PSYCHIC WONDERKIDS: PITFALLS AND PRECAUTIONS

Stanley Krippner, Ph.D.

Saybrook Institute
San Francisco, CA

The Roman Catholic Church's manual on exorcism gives specific suggestions on how to identify children who have been "possessed" by demonic forces. These children have the "ability to speak with some facility in a strange tongue or to understand it when spoken by another; the facility of divulging future and hidden events; display of powers which are beyond the subject's age and natural condition" (Karpel, 1975). It is obvious that these same "signs" could be used to identify children who are of interest to parapsychologists.

Indeed, these descriptors apply to the "psychic children" in the Peoples' Republic of China whose purported abilities gained worldwide attention in the late 1970s and early 1980s (e.g., Ebon, 1982; Jeffries, 1982). In 1979, for example, a Chinese newspaper related the story of Tang Yu who supposedly was able to place crumpled paper balls next to his ear and identify the messages that had been written on them. Soon, children from various parts of the Peoples' Republic were identified with similar "extraordinary functions of the human body" (Truzzi, 1985). Their exploits were reported by Nature Journal, a popular science magazine, and a variety of symposia and conferences were held on the topic. The filmed accounts of their exploits were shown on Chinese television. Soon the number of children with supposed "extraordinary human functions" (EHF) exceeded 2,000 (Truzzi).

In October 1981, I took a group of Saybrook students to investigate these children. Leading our tour was Shuyin Mar, of the Savant Association, Arlington, Virginia. Several members of the Parapsychological Association -- Thelma Moss, Harold Puthoff, Jerry Solfvin, and Marcello Truzzi -- joined our group.

Our first stop was in Beijing, where several of the PA members joined me for a visit to the High Energy Physics Institute, where we lectured to a group of interested scientists. Unfortunately, parapsychology had just come under attack in the PRC by a powerful Communist party theoretician, so our audience was small. Nevertheless, I noticed the celebrated astrophysicist, Qian Xue Sen, take a seat in the back row once the lights were turned off, leaving just as the program concluded.

Our first encounter with the EHF children was in a hotel lobby. The children and their parents were extremely excited, as were the local researchers. Conditions for testing and for demonstrations were chaotic. Nevertheless, the children eagerly took the canisters that we had brought from North America and attempted to identify the contents. Their attempts were unsuccessful, and the Chinese, American, and Canadian researchers started to draw simple designs on folded paper. Some of these attempts met with greater success; for example, I drew a small red star and folded it carefully before presenting it to a young girl. I hoped that this ubiquitous symbol would be a less formidable target, and I was correct. The girl identified it correctly, but the conditions were not rigorous enough to preclude the possibility of peeking. Nonetheless, it allowed our session to end on a friendly note.

We continued our investigations in Xian, the ancient Chinese capital. In Xian we met with three girls between the ages of 6 and 12. Their parents told about their successful attempts to break needles at a distance, to unscrew a pen which had been placed in a box, and to "see" internal organs. Their attempts at diagnosis for members of our group were not spectacular, although one girl "looked" at Shuyin Mar (who was missing her gall bladder and appendix) stating that she saw "empty spaces." Another member of our group suffered from arthritis and had a peg in her knee; she was diagnosed as having "some trouble with the legs" as well as "redness" in the knee (although the opposite knee was identified).

In Shanghai, we visited the editor of Nature Journal and his staff. They brought four children to our hotel for several hours of conversation and testing. When they attempted to identify the contents of sealed containers, they were almost totally unsuccessful. A picture of a light bulb was identified as "a soft rectangle" and a pictured basket as "a new round item" -- the closest of the attempts.

They were more successful on uncontrolled tests. The number "16" was written (in Chinese) on paper, folded, and presented to a child who -- after considerable effort -- identified it correctly. They even identified the colors in which the numerals had been written, e.g., "blue 5," "black 28."

At this point, I drew a design and folded the paper in a somewhat unorthodox fashion. The child seemed to place the paper under her armpit, went through considerable gyrations, which included placing her hands in front of her eyes, and eventually identified the design correctly. But when the paper was returned, I noticed that it had been unfolded and incorrectly refolded.

At the same session, Thelma Moss presented the children with a wristwatch enclosed in a box fastened by rubber bands. The watch was returned with the hands about two hours ahead of their original placement. However, one rubber band was gone and the piece of metal used to set the hands was protruding from the side of the watch. Apparently, it had been pulled out and had not been pushed back in. Close observation indicated that two of the girls worked in tandem, passing objects back and forth while shuffling on the sofa. One of the children apparently made no attempts to use trickery; he was the most unsuccessful of the young subjects.

I did my best to explain to our hosts that such behavior was injurious to their cause. If the children were ill at ease with foreign visitors, or tired from a long school day (the audiences were usually held in the evening), they should simply have refused to cooperate until conditions were optimal. At the same time, these children were receiving gifts from foreign visitors, as well as attention from adults unknown to them until they began to display purported EHF phenomena. Possible motivations for sleight of hand were not difficult to attribute to the young participants!*

Many of the scientific researchers we spoke to admitted that there were problems encountered in working with children. Their preference was adult Qigong masters, and some provocative data had been obtained with them, especially in regard to their possible ability to affect photomultiplier tube radiation (Yonjie & Hongzhang, 1982).

Our group was unable to render a positive verdict on the question of China's EHF children. Nevertheless, the enthusiasm that surrounded their newly found abilities (whether authentic or spurious) are just the milieu that often accompanies short-lived anomalous phenomena. Perhaps future investigators, both Chinese and foreign, can capitalize on this enthusiasm -- should it recur -- and engage in both field and laboratory research that is preplanned, rigorous, and yet well suited to the young girls and boys who, like those we visited, so eagerly seek adult attention and recognition.

* I have observed children bend metal in the United States, usually employing misdirection of attention and bending the spoon or fork

manually. However, at a "PK party," I noticed a quite different phenomenon. Although I saw the children exert enough physical pressure on the metal to bend it, I do not think they were aware of what they were doing. The enthusiasm of the group leader, the camaraderie of the group at the "PK party," and the excitement generated when a neighbor's spoon seems to bend is likely to induce a mild dissociation. As a result, the child ends up with a bent implement and in all honesty states that he or she did not deliberately place physical force on it. However, the effort exerted was done in a dissociated state -- one which precluded both awareness at the time and memory later.

REFERENCES

Ebon, M. (1982, February). China opens the door to the paranormal. Fate, 69-76.

Jeffries, R. J. (1982, May). Psychical research in China. A.R.E. Journal, 93-105.

Karpel, C. (1975). The rite of exorcism, New York: Berkley, 3.

Truzzi, M. (1985, January). China's psychic savants. Omni, 63-66, 78.

Yonjie, Z., & Hongzhang, X. (1982, December). Psi Research, 5-8.

This paper was presented at the 33rd Annual PA Convention, August 1990, Washington, DC, under the title A Display of Powers: Peeking at China's Psychic Children.

CHILDREN'S MEMORIES OF PREVIOUS LIVES

James G. Matlock, M.L.S.

Hunter College
New York, NY

When most of us think of past memories today, probably it is of hypnotic regressions to previous lives or past life readings done by psychics or mediums. However, many people claim to remember events from other lives while they are in their normal waking state -- and of these, the majority are children.

A child who remembers things from a previous life usually begins to speak about them when he or she is very young, perhaps as soon as he or she starts to speak, but more usually between ages 2 and 5. Some children speak a great deal about the life they remember, while others say the same few things over and over. After a few years (typically between ages 5 and 8), the children begin to talk less about the previous life, and the images seem to be fading from consciousness.

The same children often behave in ways that seem strange but are consistent with their memories; sometimes, especially if they say they died violently, they may have phobias of various sorts, and sometimes, they may have skills or aptitudes for doing things that they haven't had the opportunity to learn in their present lives. The children may also look like the people they are talking about, and they may have birthmarks or birth defects which resemble marks on the bodies of the previous persons. Such marks appear especially often in cases of violent death, and resemble the death wound the previous person suffered (Matlock, 1990; Stevenson, 1987).

We can be sure that the memories, behaviors, and physical marks aren't fantasies only when we can show that the people being talked about actually existed. Fortunately, this is one of the ways the cases of the children differ from the cases of adults and from hypnotic regressions and past life readings.

Many children give enough information -- names of people and places, along with other items -- for the persons they are talking about to be traced and identified. It then turns out that many, if not most, of the things that they have been saying are correct, and their strange behaviors and physical marks make sense. Moreover, the previous lives typically lie only a few years in the past and not far from the place the children now live, which permits them to be taken back to the place they say they have lived -- and where they recognize some people and things and ask about others.

Cases of this sort have been reported from all over the world, including Europe and the United States. There are currently some 2,500 on file at the University of Virginia Health Science Center's Division of Personality Studies alone. This is where Ian Stevenson, the pioneer and still the dean of such studies, works. Stevenson doesn't just log the cases reported to him; he investigates them in the field, talking to the children and to all witnesses to the children's statements and behaviors that he can find. Stevenson has published several volumes of detailed case reports (Stevenson, 1974, 1975, 1977, 1980, 1983), and his methods have been adopted by other researchers who have replicated his basic findings (Mills, 1989; Pasricha & Stevenson, 1979; see also Matlock, 1990).

Also, Stevenson and others have reported statistical studies of large numbers of cases. These studies have further confirmed the universality of the pattern I have described above, and they have revealed some other recurrent features.

Boys are more likely than girls to recall previous lives by a two to one margin (Stevenson, 1986). The death of the previous person occurs violently much more often than mortality statistics would lead one to expect (Stevenson, 1980, 356-357). In cases with violent deaths, the children are significantly younger, and there is a shorter time between lives than there is in cases with natural deaths (Chadha & Stevenson, 1989). A recent study has also shown that the younger the child, the more likely the memories are to have occurred spontaneously, without cues or stimuli of any sort (Matlock, 1989).

Although the cases occur in places around the world, the majority of them -- especially the majority of strong cases -- are found in cultures where there is a belief in reincarnation. Moreover, despite their overall similarity, there are variations from one culture to the next. These facts have led some critics to suggest that the cases are fantasies, the results of identifications imposed on the children by their parents (e.g., Brody, 1979).

There are several difficulties with this hypothesis, among them that persons unfamiliar with actual cases often do not have a realistic idea of what the cases are like; for example, they expect subjects to be older than they are (Pasricha, 1990). Cases with especially dramatic features may be widely known, but more typical cases usually are not known outside the community in which they occur (Barker & Pasricha, 1979). There also are cases with written records made before verifications (Stevenson & Samararatne, 1988), and these, at least, cannot be due to memories reconstructed after the fact.

Perhaps the veridical (factual) elements of the cases can be explained by the subject's ESP, but there are problems with this idea as well. For one thing, ESP alone cannot easily account for the behaviors or the birthmarks. For another, if the children are using ESP to gain information about previous lives, it is strange that they are so rarely reported to have exhibited ESP at other times. Despite a belief in Asia that such children have exceptional ESP or healing abilities, these things are no more common with them than with the general population (Stevenson, 1987). The age of the children also tells against the ESP hypothesis; if there is an upper threshold for children to exhibit ESP more often than adults, it is puberty (Palmer, 1978, 146-148), but most children who remember previous lives stop doing so at a much younger age.

There are also characteristics of the cases themselves which make them look more like memory than ESP. One is the fact that the cases change with the age of the subject; the older the subject at the time he or she first speaks about the memories, the more likely the memories are to have been stimulated by something in the environment (Matlock, 1989). Cases that begin to develop when the children are older also typically have less strong behavioral memories, and physical memories such as birthmarks and birth defects are less likely to occur (Matlock, 1988).

The children's memories tend to cluster around events of the last years, months, and days of the life they talk about; the children are particularly likely to recall the death of the previous person, but this is what they are most likely to make mistakes about. They often are better at recognizing people in photographs than they are in recognizing the same people alive, especially if some time has passed between the lives, and they often are unable to recognize places that have changed much in the interval (Matlock, 1990; Stevenson, 1987). All of these things accord better with memory than with ESP.

Finally, the memories sometimes have important developmental consequences for the children, in a way that would be unexpected if only ESP is involved. Stevenson follows his subjects for several years, and each of his case reports includes a section on the subject's later development. Generally, these suggest a pattern of pronounced verbal and behavioral memories in childhood, gradually diminishing in strength, until by middle adulthood there is only a residuum. In a few cases, however, strong identification with the previous person in childhood may interfere with personality development, and occasionally, more severe problems occur. In one case (Stevenson, 1974), a child who claimed to remember the life of his uncle, who had killed his wife, was unable to develop a mature relationship with women, and was in and out of mental hospitals (cf. Matlock, 1990, 206-207).

Other explanations sometimes suggested are that past life memory cases are examples of "genetic memory." Although it is as hypothetical as reincarnation, some such idea might explain cases in which the subject is linked to the previous person in a biological way (as when both are members of the same family), but it cannot explain the many cases in which there is no biological link, either because the families were unrelated or because the previous person died without leaving progeny. Possession is also unlikely to explain past life memory cases. In only very rare cases do subjects undergo complete alterations of personality; usually, it is as if they are struggling to fit the images in their minds in with their present circumstances, exactly what one would expect if the images were indeed memories.

Two cases will serve to illustrate some of these issues. The first case concerns my nephew, who was four at the time. I had agreed to sit with him one evening, and as soon as he came in, he told me flatly: "There aren't any ghosts." I found out later that my brother-in-law had put him up to this: Jack had been talking a lot about ghosts, and his father had suggested I might be an interesting person with whom to discuss the matter. But I didn't know this at the time, and I wasn't sure how to respond. The child was only four. I didn't want to mess up his mind by telling him that there were ghosts; but neither did I want to mess it up by telling him that there weren't any. While I was still trying to decide what to say, Jack said again: "There aren't any ghosts."

Finally, I explained that many people claimed to see ghosts, and sometimes the ghosts were able to tell them things that the people didn't know at the time; in cases like these, it was hard to say for sure that ghosts didn't exist. Jack listened with rapt attention. When I was finished, he asked whether I had ever seen a ghost. No, I admitted, I never had. Then he said: "I have seen ghosts. But they're a long way away, in Illinois."

I was stunned by this admission, because my sister had been telling me for months that Jack had been speaking of Illinois and Chicago (places he had never been) and had been saying things like, "When I was 18 I had a dart gun," or "When I was 18 I had a shirt like that." I had begged her to write these things down, but she had always resisted. He was only a child, she said. He had a very active imagination; he still mixed up his tenses and his pronouns, sometimes referring to himself in the third person.

For me, however, the implication was clear. The "ghosts" he described were consistent with what was known about much better developed cases, and there was no apparent reason for him to have said this or the other things he said, unless he had some imaged memories he was trying to convey. Other Americans had told me about the apparent past life memories of their children, or of themselves when they were children, but all these had occurred sometime in the past. Here I was confronted with a child who apparently was recalling a past life then and there. Yet I did nothing to draw him out about his ghosts. I was thinking of a case that strongly suggested that it wasn't a good idea to encourage past life memories (though neither could they be suppressed).

This was a case described by the psychotherapist Helen Wambach (1978, 5-7). A five-year-old named Peter was referred to her by a doctor who could find no physical reason for Peter's hyperactivity and inability to concentrate. To Wambach's surprise, Peter began to talk to her about the life of a policeman he seemed to be remembering. His mother said that he had begun speaking about the policeman when he was three, but she had told him not to tell stories, and he had stopped talking about them to her. The only person who would listen to him was his younger sister, but when he found Wambach a willing listener, he talked about the policeman whenever he came in for treatment.

At these times Peter calmed down and behaved normally, but unfortunately he was also becoming more absorbed in his memories. After a few months, a real policeman brought him home after he found him standing in the middle of the road, directing traffic. Peter's condition showed no improvement, and he was withdrawn from therapy soon after.

These are both American cases, and we can immediately see

similarities and differences between them and the typical Asian case I described above. The ages -- Jack was four and Peter was five -- fit the standard pattern. Their memories are also consistent with what we know of other cases. But neither boy gave enough detail about the life he seemed to recall to permit verification. In these respects they are characteristic of other American cases, which tend to be relatively weak (Stevenson, 1983a).

One clue to the reason for their weakness comes from the attitudes of the parents involved. My sister could not be brought to take Jack's statements seriously enough to write them down, and Peter's mother told him not to make up stories and forbade him to talk about his memories. It is certainly plausible that the absence of social support for past life memories in the West means that the cases are less likely to develop and less likely to come to the attention of investigators when they do develop. We know that subjects of unsolved cases stop speaking about their memories earlier than do subjects of solved cases (Cook et al., 1983), which only adds to their weakness. Interestingly, Peter's mother's efforts to suppress his memories weren't successful; in this, his experience is typical of the Asian pattern, where efforts at suppression likewise are unsuccessful (Stevenson & Chadha, 1990).

Thus, although these two cases are much weaker than the standard Asian case, in form they are similar enough to justify our grouping them with the latter. And paradoxically, these cases, weak as they are, actually provide more of a challenge to the fantasy and ESP hypotheses than do stronger cases. How would ESP explain Jack's claim to see ghosts in Illinois or his statements about what he had when he was 18? How would ESP help us to understand the pressure of Peter's memories and his apparent acting them out? If their mothers were unconsciously influencing their behaviors, why in a direction so alien to their beliefs? Was Peter only trying to get his mother's attention? Why then didn't he choose another way, when she first attempted to suppress his memories? An explanation in terms of past life memory encounters no such difficulties.

Nevertheless, no matter how suggestive the data are, reincarnation is an unlikely hypothesis from our cultural point of view. For Brody, the biggest problem with Stevenson's cases is "less with the quality of the data Stevenson adduces to support his point, than in the body of knowledge and theory that must be abandoned or radically modified in order to accept it" (1979, 770). So long as there is no plausible biological model for reincarnation, this verdict is unlikely to change.

REFERENCES

Barker, D. R. & Pasricha, S. (1979). Reincarnation cases in Fatehabad: A systematic survey in north India. Journal of Asian and African Studies, 14, 230-240.

Brody, E. B. (1979). Review of Cases of the reincarnation type. Vol. II: Ten cases in Sri Lanka by Ian Stevenson. Journal of Nervous and Mental Disease, 167, 769-774.

Chadha, N. & Stevenson, I. (1988). The correlates of violent death in cases of the reincarnation type. Journal of the Society for Psychical Research, 55, 71-79.

Cook, E. W., Pasricha, S., Samararatne, G., U Win Maung, & Stevenson, I. (1983). A review and analysis of "solved" and "unsolved" cases of the reincarnation type: II. Comparison of features of solved and unsolved cases. Journal of the American Society for Psychical Research, 77, 115-135.

Matlock, J. G. (1988). The decline of past life memory with the subject's age in spontaneous reincarnation cases. In M. L. Albertson, Dan S. Ward, Kenneth P. Freeman (Eds.), Paranormal Research (pp. 388-401). Fort Collins, CO: Rocky Mountain Research Institute.

Matlock, J. G. (1989). Age and stimulus in past life memory cases: A study of published cases. Journal of the American Society for Psychical Research, 83, 303-316.

Matlock, J. G. (1990). Past life memory case studies. In S. Krippner (Ed.), Advances in parapsychological research 6 (pp. 184-267). Jefferson, NC: McFarland.

Mills, Antonia C. (1989). A replication study: Three cases of children in northern India who are said to remember a previous life. Journal of Scientific Exploration, 3, 133-184.

Palmer, J. (1978). Extrasensory perception: Research findings. In S. Krippner (Ed.), Advances in parapsychological research 2 (pp. 59-243). NY: Plenum.

Pasricha, S. (1990). Three conjectured features of reincarnation-type cases in north India. Journal of the American Society for Psychical Research, 84, 227-234.

Pasricha, S. & Stevenson, I. (1979). A partly independent replication of cases of the reincarnation type. European Journal of Parapsychology, 3, 51-65.

Stevenson, I. (1974). Twenty cases suggestive of reincarnation, 2nd ed. Charlottesville, VA: University Press of Virginia.

Stevenson, I. (1975). Cases of the reincarnation type: Vol. I, Ten cases in India. Charlottesville, VA: University Press of Virginia.

Stevenson, I. (1977). Cases of the reincarnation type: Vol. II, Ten cases in Sri Lanka. Charlottesville, VA: University Press of Virginia.

Stevenson, I. (1980). Cases of the reincarnation type: Vol. III, Twelve cases in Lebanon and Turkey. Charlottesville, VA: University Press of Virginia.

Stevenson, I. (1983a). American children who claim to remember previous lives. Journal of Nervous and Mental Disease, 171, 742-748.

Stevenson, I. (1983b). Cases of the reincarnation type: Vol. IV, Twelve Cases in Thailand and Burma. Charlottesville, VA: University Press of Virginia.

Stevenson, I. (1986). Characteristics of cases of the reincarnation type among the Igbo of Nigeria. Journal of Asian and African Studies, 21, 204-216.

Stevenson, I. (1987). Children who remember previous lives: A question of reincarnation. Charlottesville, VA: University Press of Virginia.

Stevenson, I. & Chadha, N. (1990). Can children be stopped from speaking about previous lives? Journal of the Society for Psychical Research, 56, 82-90.

Stevenson, I. & Samararatne, G. (1988). Three new cases of the reincarnation type in Sri Lanka with written records made before verifications. Journal of Scientific Exploration, 2, 217-238.

Wambach, H. (1978). Reliving past lives. NY: Barnes and Noble.

DISCUSSION

Sally Ann Drucker, Ph.D.
Athena A. Drewes, M.A., M.S., Psy.D. Candidate
H. Kanthamani, Ph.D.
Raymond Lee, Ph.D.
Stanley Krippner, Ph.D.
James G. Matlock, M.L.S.

Drucker: What testing procedures work best with younger children or with high school children? For replicability, the type of testing could be an issue.

Drewes: I think that for younger children, the types of research that have been successful have dealt with target material that is colorful, age appropriate, using common characters of the time: Popeye, Ninja Turtles, M & M candies, other candies, balloons, stickers, things of that sort, that would be more appropriate for younger children. I think testing younger children is very much parallel to doing therapy with younger children. You need to build rapport. You need to take into consideration their shorter attention spans and their emotional needs, so that in setting up a piece of research you want to tap into their ability to use fantasy. One very interesting experiment launched a rocket and had the children imagine and use their fantasy in that. So using the natural propensity of children to get excited and involved and fantasize, along with very colorful materials and age-appropriate kinds of rewards, would work best.

Kanthamani: As far as high-school-age children are concerned, the same thing applies. Basically, you should have good rapport with the kids you are working with, and then the test material and test conditions should be relevant to them just like any other age group. Basically, I find high-school-age people to be good at any type of task that we can really apply to them. When working with a reward system, that is when we had to be more discriminating as to what would be a good reward. In most of my studies, I find they are very happy if I am giving them their personality profile back to them and am interpreting it for them. That is a reward, and then they want to come back again to do more. That taps their intellectual curiosity. They want to know who they are.

In the same way, if it is a classroom situation where you are doing group work, some of the advantages are the homogeneous group and that the high-anxiety people are in relative ease in a group situation. So we may not get the same type of correlation that we might expect in individual testing. But there is an advantage, if you are looking for overall psi scoring, to use group situations, while at the same time to build that type of rapport with a group by discussion. Sometimes, what I do is talk to them about their psi experiences and that will form a good vehicle. So how we can best test is what is most meaningful at that time.

Drucker: I have another question, for Dr. Lee, about the development of psi abilities of children in China. I know that earlier, you mentioned to me that meditation is one of the things used, and I was wondering if you could discuss that a little bit further.

Lee: While it is true that children have more psychic ability, and it is easier to learn to develop psychic ability when you are young, through practicing of Qigong meditation it is possible to maintain an ability, enhance the ability, or even develop new psychic ability, according to the theory of Qigong. And if a child has psychic ability and uses that without using Qigong meditation, that ability is going to decline. And so for instance, a psychic person I met had the ability as a child, practiced Qigong, and the ability actually improved. And interesting was that one lady, she told me that after practicing Qigong one night, while I have no way to prove whether this is true or not, she saw a ghost with a green face and long hair, who said, let's go to the mountain area and I will teach you psychic ability, assuming she would be able to improve her psychic ability. In China now they have a program to use the Qigong method and some acupuncture to develop psychic ability.

Krippner: I have a question for Dr. Lee. I know that you are in the psychology department of your university, and I was wondering what the reaction was of your colleagues when you came back and told them of these experiences.

Lee: We have a big department, of about 60 faculty members. Only one was willing to believe this type of story. All the others were skeptical and discouraged me from going to China, so actually I haven't mentioned this study to my colleagues.

QUESTIONS FROM THE AUDIENCE

Question: How has genetics entered into the question of past life memory?

Matlock: It wasn't genetics but genetic memory, which is a hypothesis some people have put forward as an alternative to these cases. What that implies is that the memories have been passed through families. The difficulties with it in the reincarnation cases is that very often there is not a biological relationship between the subject and the previous person. Typically in these cases, the better ones, there is often only a few months or few years interval and the families are unrelated. Even if they are distantly related, they could not have been related during that period. And moreover, in many cases, the previous persons died before they left any progeny and clearly they could not have passed on any memories. So those considerations are altogether apart from the fact that there is no evidence of anything like that.

Question: I have a few questions for Dr. Lee. First of all, could you tell us what was the age of the person you tested who did these extraordinary feats for you?

Lee: He was in his middle thirties. He started out as a child with these abilities.

Question: Secondly, what are the prospects of bringing him to America to undergo testing?

Lee: This person was under the protection of the highest level of the Chinese government, so it is very unlikely, because he is no longer doing this type of experiment, in the space program. He also treats the highest level of the Communist leaders. He has ability. Even if it is not possible to bring him, this lady was even more able to cooperate with scientists, and she is very willing to come here. So it is possible to bring some of them here.

Question: Finally, just a small point, with that particular trick with the bottle and the pills that came out. Did you afterwards check the number of pills in the bottle to make sure that they were the ones that had disappeared and came into your hand?

Lee: I did not. So it was not rigorous enough. However, according to the recent paper published in China, an actual study, they used a piece of glass made by a professional glass blower, put the pill inside and marked it; sometimes, they put a bug inside the glass and presealed it so that the only way you could take it out was to break the glass. So it precluded and eliminated any possibility of trickery. And some children were able to move those objects outside that glass.

Question: The trick or phenomena that you mentioned with your business cards. You stated that it was unique? Am I right in taking it that you had only one of each of those cards?

Lee: Only one. Only one of a kind. In China, too, they repeated this several times. They have the abilities to repair a broken business card or leaf. One experiment, conducted by a Chinese researcher, was considered a top secret, so it was told to me, although I did not see it, and you can believe it or not. They cut the tail of a rat, and then this particular person used a hand to cover the rat with the broken tail, and of course they used glass, and we had a camera underneath to monitor the whole process, and later actually he was able to repair that broken tail. So if that can be proved to be true, I think you can win the Nobel Prize. And that is the intention of the Chinese government now. They have a national program actually supported by the Communist government, and their intention is to win the Nobel Prize by parapsychological research.

Question: I'm not quite clear from your description of this work the degree to which what the subject was to do was really controlled by the experimenter. It sounded much like a magician's demonstration. For example, did you tell this man how many pills he was to bring out of the bottle and record what he was to do? One of the best ways to control experiments against fraud is to make sure you use a protocol against your experiment. What do you say about that?

Lee: My experiment was not rigorous enough. We need to repeat a well-controlled study. However, in China, according to a recent paper, which I did not see, they used this type of bottle with a precounted number of pills inside the bottle and also weighed it, and they asked the person to remove the pill out of it and weighed it again. In a very well-controlled laboratory study, he was able to perform that. So apparently, his psychic ability is authentic, if that is true. And there is no reason that the scientists there are going to cheat. At the least, they told me that after ten years of intensive research, all the researchers cannot prove that this was trickery, although we cannot rule out completely the use of trickery. At least 700 researchers have done intensive research over ten years. They have no reason to believe that trickery happened.

Question: I want to share two points about the Chinese psychical research. The first is about the research done with children who are psychic; as we all know it is spontaneous psychic ability. In modern Chinese parapsychological research, it is a universal finding there that when children grow up, when they reach the age of ten, their ability decreases very rapidly. That is universal. And it is widely believed that this decrease of their ability is not due to educational or sociological fact, but rather some kind of a physiological fact.

Another point is about the authority of the modern psychical research. I'd like to report on an experiment I personally performed and was seen by others. Those micro-PK facts are as quickly observed as those observed in other parts of this world, and as seen through the study of the literature. Of course from my point of view and many of yours, the micro-fact is never 100% believable, because we know no boundary of magic, and that is the question. In China, we pretty much have the same kind of enemy of parapsychology, which is the street-level psychic crime, and very unfortunately that happened several years before the psychic delegation went to China. They are not able to reach high-level subjects with researchers but only street-level performers. The report appears in the magazines there and here, the negative points that are caused by their conduct. So I hope as time goes by that Chinese scholars will do more straight experiments, hence gradually using micro-effect domain. In time, I hope more western parapsychologists will go to that country and stay with their subject, get friendly with the subject, and see something there. Thank you.

Question: I should like to say something about Dr. Lee's reports of these well-controlled experiments which you did not see but know about. Of course I do not know anything about those things, but I know that in Hungary, my country, which was rather separated from the West for a long time, there were reports of a second-hand kind from the United States, about very well-controlled experiments, for example, aliens coming from UFOs who were cut and x-rayed and their inner organs mapped, and so forth. And the people who reported them were convinced, and tried to convince everybody, that they were government-involved, very high-level, very scientific investigations in this country. So what I want to say is, in those cultures which are so apart from each other, it is very easy to get the impression that the other side does something very serious and a very big thing which can never be verified, and then if you go there, as I came here, and find what is the truth, it sometimes just disappears. So I do not know what is the case there, but I do know what is the case in my country. Thank you.

PANEL SUMMATIONS

Drucker: I was very interested in Dr. Lee' s mentioning that in China too there is the common belief that children are more psychic and then lose the ability as they grow up. This is a cross-cultural concept that we find here as well.

Drewes: I would like to repeat what I said earlier, that children are particularly under-utilized as a subject pool. And I would like to encourage us all to perhaps take a second look at using this population more thoroughly and systematically and maybe applying downward in some way some of the more successful adult studies, such as Ganzfeld, and even using computers with the teenagers, which might tap more into the developmental component. And further, to look into some more longitudinal types of studies that would give us the opportunity to see what psi does as children get older.

Kanthamani: As far as high school students are concerned, I don't think there is any doubt that we have used them plenty in our research. And if our working hypothesis is that psi is normally distributed, and it is seen among all, it doesn't exclude any age group. And the reason for using high school students is that because they are easily available and congenial in many experiments, and particularly when we use them in classroom studies, there are advantages. It can certainly be continued. But as far as Ganzfeld and work like that is concerned, I would be very cautious in inviting them to participate, mainly from the standpoint of their welfare. It is an intensive procedure and people of that age are vulnerable for many fantasies and effects of that, and I would not really recommend using them for Ganzfeld, except in rare cases when the child is either accompanied by a parent or for any other special reason. One point comes to mind which we have sometimes dealt with in our research, but not extensively, is the informed consent issue with younger children. How best we can really adhere to it is very important in all research aspects, and more so when you go down the scale with younger children. With high school students, mainly what we do is take the teacher's consent as the main focus, and if anyone does not want to be part of it, they can drop out of it. A simple consent like that. If any intrusive procedures are going to be used, one has to be careful on that ground.

Krippner: Well, I think that one variable we have to keep in mind is that of the child's agenda in all of this. Their agendas are going to be much different from ours. We want to obtain data.

We want to get information about potential psychic functioning, but children might simply like the attention. They might like the rewards that they get for this performance. And we might think in terms of B.F. Skinner, who died yesterday. As most of you know, this is a matter of rewards and punishment. The children in China back in 1981, coming from a mass society where very few children are singled out for anything, were getting attention from westerners and were getting gifts from westerners. Even though the gifts we gave them were very simple, like ballpoint pens, these ballpoint pens were marks of great status among their peers and little marks that they could take to school that would give them more attention. So you can hardly blame them for trying to keep up getting all this reinforcement by whatever means that were available. By the time we left they were getting attention from teachers who identified them and sent them to these special classes, and every year now there is a Congress or Convention where these children gather and in some provinces in China there are provincial conventions. So I think the whole matter of agendas and reinforcement has to be very carefully considered when working with children.

Lee: When I said that China has a national program to study parapsychology, we have to remember that China is a big country and support by the top government official is not policy. Some government official has to protect that program. The majority of the scientists are skeptical, but at the least China has a national program supported by some branches of government agencies. So you have to be careful about this. It is not supported by the whole nation, but at least they have a national program. And it is psychic ability demonstrated in my study, only I say that it cannot be conclusively proven. We must keep a skeptical view, a cautious view, and then we need to do more vigorous study. However, the stakes are high. Apparently more vigorous and more well-controlled government studies are urgently needed in this country. And I think we can bring some of those psychic people here and prove those abilities. Maybe we will be able to stimulate interest in this country or generate more response so we can have a more positive future.

Matlock: I am pleased that children's past life memories were included on this panel because they are often left out in treatment of children in parapsychology. The status of these cases is clearly different than the status of most of the other material we have been dealing with. We would all agree that ESP and PK are established. It is not so widely agreed that past life memories are established. And yet I think we have come to the point over the last 30 years, principally through the work of Ian Stevenson, that we can move past the proof stage to the process work and begin to explore ways in which that work can relate to other areas of parapsychology and other areas of psychology, and perhaps even further to broader areas of science. I am beginning to toy with ways that we can begin to understand these cases in terms of biology and genetics. My studies in anthropology are teaching me a lot about physical anthropology, which gets very much into genetics and so I'm beginning to do some thinking along those lines. There are a number of ways we can go with this. One is developmental issues: beginning to look at long-term effects of children with these memories, the impact of these memories on these children as they grow. I'm beginning to think more seriously about the ways in which they relate to ESP. That is another way.

ANNOTATED BIBLIOGRAPHY

Clairvoyance

Telepathy

Precognition

Psychokinesis

Poltergeists

Reincarnation

Miscellaneous

JOURNALS CONSULTED

American Journal of Diseases in Children
American Journal of Psychiatry
Anabiosis
Anthropologica
British Journal of Psychical Research
British Journal of Psychology
British Journal of Statistical Psychology
Christian Parapsychologist
Contributions to Asian Studies
Corrective Psychiatry
Critical Care Medicine
European Journal of Parapsychology
Indian Journal of Parapsychology
Indian Journal of Psychiatry
International Journal of Comparative Sociology
International Journal of Parapsychology
Journal of Anthropological Research
Journal of Asian and African Studies
Journal of Heredity
Journal of Indian Psychology
Journal of Learning
Journal of Mental Science
Journal of Nervous and Mental Disease
Journal of Parapsychology
Journal of Psychological Researches
Journal of Psychology
Journal of Religion and Psychical Research
Journal of Scientific Exploration
Journal of the American Society for Psychical Research
Journal of the Society for Psychical Research
New Age Journal
New England Journal of Parapsychology
Omega
Parapsychology Review
Perceptual and Motor Skills
Proceedings of the Society for Psychical Research
Psi Comunicacion
PSI Research
Psychoanalytic Quarterly
Psychoanalytic Review

Psychological Reports
Quarterly Transactions of the British College of Psychic Science
Research Letter of the Parapsychological Division of the Psychological Laboratory of the University of Utrecht
Science Education
Suicide and Life Threatening Behavior

I. CLAIRVOYANCE

I. CLAIRVOYANCE

A. Pre-school/elementary age (infancy to 12 years)

1. Anderson, M. L. (1957). **Clairvoyance and teacher-pupil attitudes in fifth and sixth grades.** Journal of Parapsychology, 21, 1-12.

Clairvoyance experiments were conducted with two fifth-grade classes (56 students) and two sixth-grade classes (57 students) using teachers as agents. Prior to the tests, each teacher gave his/her attitude toward each student; students independently rated the teacher. Over 446 runs and 11,150 calls were given. Results showed that students liking the teacher scored above chance, those disliking the teacher scored below chance, and students who liked and were liked by the teacher scored positively. Those students who disliked and in turn were disliked by the teacher scored negatively. The difference between the latter two groups was significant.

2. Anderson, M. L. (1959). **The relationship between level of ESP scoring and student class grade.** Journal of Parapsychology, 23, 1-18.

The article examines 10 research studies carried out with 1,228 students at nine different grade levels (fifth grade to junior college, with the majority high schoolers). A statistically significant relationship was found between ESP scores and grades; students who received high grades (A and B) tended to average above chance on ESP tests, while students with lower grades (D and E) scored below chance. The C students did not show ESP. Teacher-pupil attitudes were also analyzed, with the most striking negative ESP deviation by the D and E students who disliked their teachers. Those D and E grade students with a favorable teacher attitude scored close to chance.

3. Anderson, M. L. (1960). **A year's testing program with a class of public school pupils.** Journal of Parapsychology, 24, 314.

Two clairvoyance and one precognition test (launching of a missile) were administered by a teacher to her fourth- and fifth-grade pupils. The two clairvoyance series together yielded significant results. The precognitive test was slightly below chance.

4. Anderson, M. L. (1966). **The use of fantasy in testing for extrasensory perception.** Journal of the American Society for Psychical Research, 60, 150-163.

This reviews three separate studies conducted with elementary school children. The first involved a clairvoyance and precognition test in which 32 students "tuned-in" on the "music of outer space." The second had 28 students who mentally "launched" a mythical missile. The third, involving the entire elementary school, was a clairvoyance test around mentally launching, orbiting, and recovering a space capsule. This last test explored the relationship of ESP scoring and creativity as assessed by teacher ratings. Each study had significant results.

5. Anderson, M. L. & Gregory, E. (1959). **A two-year program of tests for clairvoyance and precognition with a class of public school pupils.** Journal of Parapsychology, 23, 149-177.

Fifth-grade students (32), having scored well on previous ESP tests, were chosen for a two-year experiment. Clairvoyance tests were given the first year, yielding nonsignificant positive results. The second-year tests were precognitive in nature and used the same class (now sixth grade) and teacher. Total scores gave positively significant results. Variations in scoring from session to session also yielded significant results.

6. Anderson, M. L. & McConnell, R. A. (1962). **Fantasy testing for ESP in a fourth- and fifth-grade class.** Journal of Psychology, 52, 491-503. (Also abstracted in Journal of Parapsychology, 1962, 26, 135.

Twenty-eight pupils of a combined fourth- and fifth-grade class were tested for clairvoyance and precognition through purposeful fantasy in the launching of a rocket. A total of 6,620 guesses made in eight sessions yielded overall significant results (p = .03).

7. Banerjee, H. N. (1962). **ESP tests between mothers and children.** Journal of Parapsychology, 26, 268.

Twenty mother-child pairs (children ages 4 1/2 to 6) in India were tested, using mothers as the clairvoyant agents. Two hundred runs yielded highly significant results ($p = .00002$). NOTE: The possibility of fraud in this experiment has been raised by parapsychologists. (See book review by K. R. Rao and correspondence listed below.)

8. Banerjee, H. N. (1962-63). **ESP investigation between the mother and child.** Indian Journal of Parapsychology, 4, 87-93.

Twenty children (age 5) were given a session of ten trials with the mother as agent. Results were significant. NOTE: The possibility of fraud in this experiment has been raised by parapsychologists. (See book review by K. R. Rao and correspondence listed below.)

9. Banerjee, H. N. (1961-62). **Seemi technique in ESP tests.** Indian Journal of Parapsychology, 3, 39-46.

Mother agents were used in a clairvoyance experiment with 20 children (age 5). Results were significant. NOTE: The possibility of fraud in this experiment has been raised by parapsychologists. (See book review by K. R. Rao and correspondence listed below.)

10. Banerjee, H. N. (1963). **Seemi technique in ESP.** Journal of Parapsychology, 27, 59.

This is a reprinting of the above experiment, whereby statistically significant results were obtained in a clairvoyance experiment with 20 mother-child pairs. NOTE: The possibility of fraud in this experiment has been raised by parapsychologists. (See book review by K. R. Rao and correspondence listed below.)

NOTE: Book Review and Correspondence

Rao, K. R. (1964). [Review of Five years report of Seth Sohan Lal Memorial Institute of Parapsychology, by S. C. Mukherjee. Sri Ganganagar (India): Seth Sohan Lal Memorial Institute of Parapsychology, 1962]. Journal of Parapsychology, 28, 59-62.

This reviews in depth the ESP research with mother-child groups by Banerjee. The validity of the results are questioned, as Banerjee was unable to replicate results at the Parapsychology Laboratory in Durham, N.C. A copy of Banerjee's record sheets of additional studies yielded no evidence of common effects expected in ESP results: declines, U-curves. Additional eyewitness reports of the research procedure cast doubt over the experiments conducted and the results. Correspondence on this review by J. G. Pratt, I. Stevenson, H. N. Banerjee, and K. R. Rao is included in the Journal of Parapsychology, 1964, 28, 258-273.

11. Banham, K. M. (1966). **Temporary high scoring by a child subject.** Journal of Parapsychology, 30, 106-113.

An eight-year-old boy made significantly high ESP scores in six testing sessions over a three-month period. After an interval of seven months, he returned for additional testing, but obtained only chance results. Changes in motivation appear to have been responsible for decline in scoring.

12. Banham, K. M. (1968). **Follow-up study of a high scoring subject.** Journal of Parapsychology, 32, 143.

A series of five gamelike matching procedures were used in an informal testing of a nine-year-old boy who had previously achieved significantly high ESP scores. The child showed interest and self-confidence in only one of the tests in the new series of experiments, and on this one test alone he scored significantly.

13. Berger, R. E. (1989). **Discussion: A critical examination of the Blackmore PSI experiments.** Journal of the American Society for Psychical Research, 83, 123-144.

Blackmore's psi experiments' data base (two experiments with young children) is examined and found to have discrepancies between unpublished reports and published counterparts. Blackmore's claims that her data base shows no evidence of psi are called unfounded. Berger states that no conclusions at all can be drawn from her data base.

Blackmore, S. J. **A critical response to Rick Berger,** 145-154. Blackmore finds Berger's accusations unfounded; where she failed to replicate Spinelli's results with children, she indicates problems with Spinelli's reportage and statistics.

Berger, R. E. **Reply to Blackmore's "A critical response to Rick Berger,"** 155-157. Berger refutes points made by Blackmore.

14. Blackmore, S. (1980). **A study of memory and ESP in young children.** Journal of the Society for Psychical Research, 50, 501-520.

The literature on ESP in children is reviewed and found to show little systematic evidence of a relationship between ESP and age. In a pilot study, 19 playgroup children (ages 3-6) were tested for clairvoyance and GESP, with different colored candies as targets. Results were not significant. In the main experiment, subjects were 48 children from three playgroups (ages 3-5). Children were given memory and preference tests. Targets were colored pictures on white cards. Children took turns as sender and receiver. Results showed no significant correlation of either memory or age of the child with ESP.

15. Bottrill, J. (1969). **Effects of motivation on ESP.** Journal of Parapsychology, 33, 70.

Forty young boys scored significantly higher than forty adults ($p < .01$) in guessing which of five small doors contained an object (button or a reward). When tests involved a reward (candy for children, cigarettes for adults), scores were better ($p < .05$).

16. Chauvin, R. (1959). **Influence of the position of the subject in relation to the test cards upon ESP results.** Journal of Parapsychology, 23, 257-266.

One adult and seven children (ages 8-14) called targets (numbers 1 or 2) laid out in a variety of positions (in front, behind, overhead, below, or at angle). Total number of hits was nonsignificant. Additional analyses of data are discussed.

17. Eisenbud, J., Hassel, L., Keely, H., & Sawrey, W. (1960). **A further study of teacher-pupil attitudes and results on clairvoyance tests in the fifth and sixth grades.** Journal of the American Society for Psychical Research, 54, 72-80.

Seven fifth- and sixth-grade classes (175 students) were given clairvoyance tests after the teacher's attitude toward each pupil was noted and the pupils rated the teacher. No significant difference was found; the tests failed to replicate the Anderson-White experiments. Explanations are offered.

18. Fisk, G. W. (1951-52). **ESP experiments with an infant as subject.** Journal of the Society for Psychical Research, 36, 502-504.

A down-through clairvoyance experiment was conducted with a 14-month-old girl, yielding significant results. Results from a cross-channel test yielded only chance results.

19. Foster, A. A. (1943). **ESP tests with American Indian children: A comparison of methods.** Journal of Parapsychology, 7, 94-103.

Fifty American Indian children (ages 6-20) in Canada were given ESP tests by their teacher. Screened Touch Matching vs. presentation of ESP cards behind an opaque screen were utilized for the ESP test. The latter method gave significant results, while the former technique gave only chance scores.

20. Freeman, J. A. (1962). **A testing technique for preschool children.** Journal of Parapsychology, 26, 267-268.

Thirteen kindergarten children were told ESP test squares were flower boxes and that seeds had been planted in the boxes. They were given five crayons matching the five colors of the flowers and asked to record what color they thought would grow. Overall scores were not significant. No difference between group test scoring and individual test scoring was found. A marginally significant difference between boys' and girls' scoring was noted (p = .027).

21. Freeman, J. A. (1966). **A sequel report on a high-scoring child.** Journal of Parapsychology, 30, 39-47.

A nine-year-old girl reported to have unusual ability to guess playing cards was informally tested over a three-year period. Her scoring, which at first was extremely high, gradually dwindled to chance level.

22. Giesler, P. V. (1985). **An attempted replication of Winkelman's ESP and socialization research** [Summary]. In R. White & J. Solfvin (Eds.), Research in Parapsychology 1984 (pp. 24-27). Metuchen, NJ: Scarecrow Press.

Thirty-six children living in Brazil (ages 8-16; 18 males, 18 females), were given 30 trials of a clairvoyance (CV) task,

40 PK trials, and a formal math test with educational years controlled. The CV test involved guessing which of three colored candy balls out of nine total would be selected; the reward given was a similar candy from a different bag. The PK task required influencing a random-event generator to light either one of two light bulbs on its machine, with one series having a small statue of a regional deity behind one bulb. Overall PK and CV scores were negative and nonsignificant, thus not confirming Winkelman's results. CV, PK, and math correlations were nonsignificant.

23. Goldstone, G. (1959). **Two repetitions of the Anderson-White investigation of teacher-pupil attitudes and clairvoyance test results. Part II: Grade-school tests.** Journal of Parapsychology, 23, 208-213.

This is an attempted replication of the Anderson-White experiments with 160 grade school pupils (79 in fifth grade, 81 in sixth grade) and six teachers. Results were nonsignificant. There were 800 runs (20,000 calls). (See Deguisne, A., 1959. **Two repetitions of the Anderson-White investigation of teacher-pupil attitudes and clairvoyance test results. Part I: High school tests.** Journal of Parapsychology, 23, 196-207.)

24. Hsin, C. & Lei, M. (1983). **Study of the extraordinary function of the human body in China** [Summary]. In W. G. Roll, J. Beloff, & R. White (Eds.), Research in Parapsychology 1982 (pp. 278-282). Metuchen, NJ: Scarecrow Press.

This summary of psi phenomena research in China was presented at a parapsychology conference in 1982. Experiments with over 70 children (age 10) showed that a considerable proportion could recognize written Chinese characters held next to their ears, without visual contact.

25. Jampolsky, G. G. & Haight, M. J. (1975). **A pilot study of ESP in hyperkinetic children.** [Summary]. In J. D. Morris, W. G. Roll, & R. L. Morris (Eds.), Research in Parapsychology 1974 (pp. 13-15). Metuchen, NJ: Scarecrow Press.

Two groups of children (ages 9-13) were tested for clairvoyance. One group had 10 hyperkinetic males, and the other group had 10 normal males and females. Each performed 192 runs of 25 trials (4,800 total trials each) on a four-choice

ESP machine, as well as two clairvoyance runs using 50 envelopes containing black or white paper targets. Overall results were nonsignificant for each group. Additional analyses are discussed.

26. Johnson, M. (1970). **Teacher-pupil relationship and ESP scoring.** Journal of Parapsychology, 34, 277.

A sixth-grade class performed two 25-trial runs with ESP cards. The first run was a clairvoyance task, while the second run used blank cards and was a precognitive task. The teacher-agent rated students on intelligence, extraversion-introversion, degree of rapport with teacher, and anxiety-proneness. The clairvoyance run yielded positive but nonsignificant results. The precognitive run yielded positive, significant results ($p < .01$). The correlation between teacher's ratings and students' performance was in the expected direction but nonsignificant.

27. Johnson, M., Cronquist, A., Danielsson, B. I., & Mondejar, A. (1972). **A test of clairvoyance especially designed for children.** Research Letter of the Parapsychological Division of the Psychological Laboratory of the University of Utrecht, 9-15.

Fifty-two children (ages 3-7) were divided into 26 paired groups, with one group having a parent-agent and the other an outsider-agent. Rewards of candy, pencils, and balloons were given. Children with a parent as the main experimenter had a higher degree of success than the group having an outsider-agent. Results were nonsignificant for the outsider-agent group.

28. Kanthamani, H., Khilji, A., & Perlstrom, J. (1986). **Social facilitation and ESP performance among children** [Summary]. In D. Weiner & D. Radin (Eds.), Research in Parapsychology 1985 (pp. 44-49). Metuchen, NJ: Scarecrow Press.

Preliminary and main clairvoyance experiments were conducted with a total of 72 children (ages 6-10), using four colored cartoon character targets. Two social facilitation conditions entailed: 1) the subjects working as a team to score a hit, and 2) each subject working independently for a hit. Rewards were colorful stickers. Results of the preliminary study were nonsignificant. The main experiment showed that regardless of the sex pairs, the cooperative and competitive conditions were significant. Hits in the cooperative condition were also significant.

29. Kiang, T. (1982). **Sighted hands: A report on experiments with four Chinese children to test their ability to see colour pictures and symbols with their hands.** Journal of the Society for Psychical Research, 51, 304-308.

Four children (ages 1-12; 3 girls, 1 boy) were tested in China for clairvoyance, using colored picture cards and symbols in sealed containers. In three experiments, the subjects were able to give reliable descriptions of their targets. A fourth experiment, which did not allow for physical contact, could not be completed due to subject fatigue. No statistical analyses were conducted.

30. Lamacchia, C. & Venske, J. (1969). **ESP tests among gifted, normal, and retarded children.** Journal of Parapsychology, 33, 162.

Ninety students of different intellectual levels were divided equally into three groups: one of educable mentally retarded, one of normal children, and one of gifted children. Each group was tested for clairvoyance. A total of 150 runs with ESP cards yielded gifted students scoring significantly higher ($p = .01$) than either normal or educable mentally retarded children.

31. Murray, D. M. (1983). **The effect of schooling on the manifestation of clairvoyant abilities among Isnag children of the Northern Philippines** [Summary]. In W. G. Roll, J. Beloff, & R. White (Eds.), Research in Parapsychology 1982 (pp. 245-248). Metuchen, NJ: Scarecrow Press.

Subjects were 36 children (ages 8-16), four children per category. The clairvoyance test consisted of 30 three-target trials using 60 red, yellow, and green candies. A math skills test was also administered. T-test results were nonsignificant for clairvoyance. Multiple regression analysis results indicated that males had statistically higher clairvoyance scores than females ($p < .05$). This study failed to replicate Winkelman's (1981) study showing significant negative correlations between age and clairvoyance.

32. Musso, J. R. (1965). **ESP experiments with primary school children.** Journal of Parapsychology, 29, 115-121.

A total of 302 primary school children (grades 1-6 in Buenos Aires) were evaluated to see: 1) whether sheep-goat attitudes affected ESP scoring, 2) if there was a difference in scoring when the child's teacher was agent, and 3) if the child's grade had any effect. The sheep-goat analysis gave significantly positive scores for sheep and borderline negative scores for goats. There was a significant difference between these latter two groups.

33. Nash, C. B. & Buzby, D. E. (1965). **Extrasensory perception of identical and fraternal twins.** Journal of Heredity, 56, 52-54. (Reprinted in Journal of Parapsychology, 1967, 31, 84.)

Twenty-five pairs of twins (11 identical, 14 fraternal) were given clairvoyance tests with ESP cards. Ages ranged from five to thirteen years, with a mean age of seven. The first three runs had the mother as sender, and the last six runs had the twins alternate as sender. Identical twins scored in the negative direction, while fraternal twins scored in the positive direction. The difference between the two scores was nonsignificant. Females scored higher than males, although overall results were nonsignificant.

34. Peretti, P. O. & Gierkey, J. (1978). **Clairvoyance performance in youth.** Journal of Psychological Researches, 22, 21-32.

Clairvoyance testing was conducted individually using Zener cards on 163 children (ages 4-18). There were seven equal groups for age and sex, with three runs for a total of 75 trials. Significant results were found for girls in the 6.1- to 8-year, 8.1- to 10-year, and 12.1- to 14-year groups. Significance levels and statistical methods used were not reported.

35. Puthoff, H. E. (1983). **Report on investigations into "Exceptional Human Body Function" in the People's Republic of China** [Summary]. In W. G. Roll, J. Beloff, & R. A. White (Eds.), Research in Parapsychology 1982 (pp. 275-278). Metuchen, NJ: Scarecrow Press.

This recounts a tour of China in 1981 made by American and Canadian scientists to explore Chinese psi phenomena

(Exceptional Human Body Function--EHBF) in children and attend a related parapsychology conference. At the conference were 14 children who demonstrated EHBF skills. Phenomena included the ability to "read" written material placed in physical contact with the children's ears.

36. Rhine, J. B. (1969). **Position effects in psi test results.** Journal of Parapsychology, 33, 136-157.

Sixteen adults (ages 21-49) showed effects more markedly than fourteen children (ages 5-13 years) of position effect-hit frequency (declines and U-curves).

37. Rhine, L. E. (1937). **Some stimulus variations in extrasensory perception with child subjects.** Journal of Parapsychology, 1, 102-113.

Over 14,200 trials with 17 children (ages 3-15) were conducted to see the effect upon ESP when size of card and number of cards presented at one time were varied. Large card symbols were mixed with small ones and matched by the subject without the subject's knowing which was which. In other cases, cards bearing five symbols were mixed with others showing only one. Nonsignificant results were obtained, although total scores were indicative of ESP. Some suggestions are given for using children as subjects.

38. Rhine, L. E. (1956). **The relationship of agent and percipient in spontaneous telepathy.** Journal of Parapsychology, 20, 1-32. (Children mentioned intermittently on pp. 10, 12-17, 29-30.)

The article recounts several spontaneous child telepathy cases and one child clairvoyance case.

39. Rilling, M. E. & Adams, J. Q. (1959). **Teacher-pupil attitudes and clairvoyance test scores in the college and elementary classroom.** Journal of Parapsychology, 23, 291.

An attempt was made to replicate the Anderson-White tests using a group of fourth- and fifth-grade pupils (155 pupils) and a group of college students (176 students). ESP results were nonsignificant for either group. Elementary school data revealed directional similarities to the Anderson-White experiment. The college results showed that when the professor was positive toward ESP, the class tended to score above chance, and the class tended to score below chance when the professor was negative toward ESP.

40. Rilling, M. E., Adams, J. Q., & Pettijohn, C. (1962). **A summary of some clairvoyance experiments conducted in classroom situations.** Journal of the American Society for Psychical Research, 56, 125-130.

Part I: An attempt to replicate the Anderson-White experiments with 30 fifth-grade pupils on clairvoyance tasks yielded nonsignificant results. Part II: A total of 155 students in fourth- and fifth-grade classes, as well as 176 college introductory psychology students, did four clairvoyance runs each in two sessions. ESP results from both groups for attitude of subject toward teacher were not significant. None of the analyses relating teacher-pupil attitudes to ESP scoring level were significant.

41. Rongliang, Z. (1982). **Parapsychology in China** [Summary]. In W. G. Roll, R. Morris, & R. A. White (Eds.), Research in Parapsychology 1981 (p. 180). Metuchen, NJ: Scarecrow Press.

Many discoveries of children with paranormal abilities have surfaced since 1979. Several hundred children (ages 9-14) have been identified, with 30 to 40 children having unusually strong clairvoyant, telepathic, and psychokinetic powers. Children with clairvoyance are reported to see "vital force" released from the Qi-gong master's body.

42. Ross, A. O., Murphy, G., & Schmeidler, G. R. (1952). **The spontaneity factor in extrasensory perception.** Journal of the American Society for Psychical Research, 46, 14-16.

Thirty subjects (ages 4 1/2 to 8) in preschool and primary classes were observed during structured play and were rated for: zest, originality, constraint, rigidity, perseveration, and reflectiveness. Teachers also rated children on some factors. Screened Touch Matching for card-calling clairvoyance was conducted with groups of high- vs. low-spontaneity children. High-spontaneity children showed positive deviation from chance, while the low-spontaneity children showed a negative deviation. The difference between means was significant at the .09 level.

43. Sailaja, P. & Rao, P. V. (1978). **Response patterns and psi scoring.** Journal of Parapsychology, 42, 304-312.

Two series of studies, using 50 female subjects (ages 12-14 years) and 49 subjects (ages 10-12 years), attempted to replicate findings by Kanthamani and Rao (1975). The number of meaningful words subjects checked as ESP responses over alternative meaningless words was felt to be a good predictor of how well subjects would do on the clairvoyance part of the test. In the first series, there was significant correlation ($p < .01$) between the number of meaningful words checked and ESP scores obtained. The results of the second series were nonsignificant. Nonsignificant results overall were found between the first and second series on relationship between ESP scores and subjects' expectation of success.

44. Shargal, S. (1987). **Children's ESP scores in relation to age** [Summary]. In D. Weiner & R. Nelson (Eds.), Research in Parapsychology 1986 (pp. 51-53). Metuchen, NJ: Scarecrow Press.

Normal first graders (15) were tested on two 15-target clairvoyance tests with significant scores ($p < .025$). Another clairvoyance study was conducted with 115 first-, third-, and fifth-grade students who were equally distributed by grade and sex. Results showed that first graders scored better than the older children ($p = .025$) on both the ESP task and when grade and body boundary scores were a factor. The hypothesis that ESP would decline with age was proven.

45. Shields, E. (1962). **Comparison of children's guessing ability with personality characteristics.** Journal of Parapsychology, 26, 200-210.

Children (ages 6-14) referred because of behavioral, learning, or emotional difficulties took part in two experiments. In the first, twenty-one children were given a battery of personality and intellectual tests for classification as either "withdrawn" or "not withdrawn." An ESP game using Popeye picture cards was administered, with half the runs for clairvoyance and the other half for GESP. The withdrawn group scored marginally significantly below chance. The not-withdrawn group scored significantly above chance. The difference in rate of scoring between the two groups was also significant. In the second experiment, 98 children were divided into withdrawn and not-withdrawn groups and given a matching ESP test. The withdrawn group was slightly, but not significantly, above chance, and the not-withdrawn group was above chance to a significant degree. The total combined not-withdrawn group yielded a significant difference compared to the withdrawn group. Additional analyses were conducted.

46. Shields, E. (1976). **Severely mentally retarded children's psi ability** [Summary]. In J. D. Morris, W. G. Roll, & R. L. Morris (Eds.), Research in Parapsychology 1975 (pp. 135-139). Metuchen, NJ: Scarecrow Press.

Twenty-five children (ages 7-21) diagnosed as trainable mentally retarded (IQs 30-63), having Down's syndrome (IQs 21-71), and having no medical diagnosis (IQs 32-73) were tested for telepathy and clairvoyance. All three groups scored significantly on telepathy tasks. Clairvoyance scores approached significance. Neither telepathy nor clairvoyance scores correlated with age or IQ, and the three diagnostic groups did not differ markedly from each other.

47. Shields, E. & Mulders, C. (1975). **Pleasant vs. unpleasant targets on children ESP tests and their relationship to personality tests.** Journal of Parapsychology, 39, 165-175.

Forty-six boys and fourteen girls (ages 6-13) were divided into groups of attention-seekers and attention-avoiders. Each was shown 75 picture cards, had to choose five pleasant and five unpleasant ones, and then had to match the experimenter's concealed target row of pleasant and unpleasant cards. Attention-seekers scored significantly higher than attention-avoiders. No significant difference was found between deeply disturbed and not deeply disturbed children.

48. Teng, L. C. (1981). **Letter.** Journal of the Society for Psychical Research, 51 181-183.

A report on a 12-year-old boy with "exceptional faculties" -- when paper balls with writing on them are put in his ears, he can write down the balls' written contents on separate paper. The boy describes seeing images of the writing, which appear more quickly when he is in a good mood and warmed up.

49. Vasse, C. & Vasse, P. (1958). **ESP tests with French first grade school children.** Journal of Parapsychology, 22, 187-203.

Clairvoyance tests were administered to 28 first-grade pupils in a French school. Three series of tests were made: the first near the end of the school year, the second at the beginning of the next school year, and the third at the end of the second year. All tests were conducted during recess periods, and only those pupils who wished to give up their play activities were used as subjects. Five pictures drawn and selected by children and five regular ESP symbols were used as targets, in both a matching technique and a technique in which cards were called "up through" the pack. Highly significant results were obtained with both procedures in two series conducted near the end of the school year. The series conducted at the beginning of the year yielded scores that were below chance.

50. Winkelman, M. (1981). **The effects of schooling and formal education upon extrasensory abilities** [Summary]. In W. G. Roll & J. Beloff (Eds.), Research in Parapsychology 1980 (pp. 26-29). Metuchen, NJ: Scarecrow Press.

Clairvoyance and PK tests were performed on an evenly divided group of 40 children (ages 7-14) in Mexico. A variety of clairvoyance tests included 20 trials using three colors of gum, marbles, and crayons. PK tests involved the use of marbles and dice. Additional educational tests were given (math, reading, memory, and Children's Embedded Figures Test). Clairvoyance tests showed no individual or overall significance. PK with marbles was nonsignificant, while PK with dice was positively significant ($p < .05$). Negative correlations with schooling, ages, and clairvoyance were significant.

51. Winkelman, M. (1981). **The effect of formal education on extrasensory abilities: The Ozolco Study.** Journal of Parapsychology, 45, 321-336.

Three experiments assessed whether or not an increase in formal education inhibits ESP abilities. Subjects were 29 children from a rural Mexican village, ages 8-14 years, with 0-7 years of education. Clairvoyance testing with candy yielded significant results ($p < .005$), while use of marbles in clairvoyance testing was nonsignificant. Precognitive testing with candy was significant at the .05 level, while precognition using marbles was nonsignificant. PK testing using marbles yielded $p < .1$. There were no strong significant differences between males and females. Additional testing of field independence, conservation, math, and years of schooling were correlated.

Total ESP correlated negatively with math ($p < .02$), schooling ($p < .03$), conservation, field independence, and age. Similar negative correlations were found with clairvoyance and precognition testing. PK correlated positively with age ($p < .006$).

52. Zingrone, N. (1985). **The Southeastern Regional Parapsychological Association Conference.** *Journal of Parapsychology*, *49*, 257-264.

The article reviews the various papers presented at the above conference. Included was **Effects of motivational sets on ESP scores in children: A preliminary report,** by A. Khilji and H. Kanthamani. A simple ESP test using a specially designed deck with cartoon characters was given to 12 pairs of children (ages 5-10). Cooperative and competitive conditions were given, with colorful stickers as rewards. Significant results were found for the competition condition only. Post hoc analysis yielded significant results, with members of opposite-sex pairs in the cooperative condition only. Also refer to earlier entry, this section, Kanthamani, H., Khilji, A., & Perlstrom, J. (1986).

B. Junior high schoolers (13-15 years)

53. Carpenter, J. C. (1971). **The differential effect and hidden target differences consisting of erotic and neutral stimuli.** Journal of the American Society for Psychical Research, 65, 204-214.

Two exploratory experiments are reported. Both experiments employ an erotic-neutral target difference with blind matching. The first experiment with 19 junior high schoolers resulted in a significant interaction between target type and anxiety level (measured by Taylor Manifest Anxiety Scale), ($p < .01$). High-anxiety students showed psi-hitting on neutral and psi-missing on erotic targets. Mid- and low-anxiety students scored the opposite. The second experiment classified 31 junior high students as sheep or goats, with sex guilt measured by the Mosher Guilt Scale. Sheep scored higher than goats and had significantly lower sex-guilt scores than did goats. High-guilt goat subjects scored lower than low-guilt subjects on erotic targets than on neutral ones, while low-guilt goats scored conversely. Results indicate that differential scoring can occur even when subjects do not know that a target difference exists. The effect of target difference appears related to personality differences.

54. Chauvin, R. (1961). **ESP and size of target symbols.** Journal of Parapsychology, 25, 185-189.

Microfilmed and normal-sized targets were tested on four children (ages 10-14) for a total of 1,296 trials. The first of two runs resulted in negatively statistically significant scores for small-sized vs. normal-sized targets. Overall difference was marginally significant.

55. Jones, J. N. & Feather, S. R. (1969). **Relationship between reports of psi experiences and subject variance.** Journal of Parapsychology, 33, 311-319.

After listening to a talk on ESP, groups of high-school and junior high-school subjects filled out a five-item psi experience questionnaire and took an ESP test. Two preliminary series (51 high schoolers) and a pilot study showed nonsignificant results. A post hoc analysis indicated that subjects with the greater number of ESP experiences had a greater variance in scoring than those who had fewer experiences. A first confirmatory series (53 high schoolers) gave results that were in the same direction ($p < .025$). A second confirmatory series (276 junior high schoolers) was at chance level. The difference between the two series gave suggestive results ($p < .05$).

56. Kanthamani, B. K. (1966). **ESP and social stimulus.** *Journal of Parapsychology*, *30*, 31-38.

Ten pairs of junior high students (ages 13-15) were tested in a gamelike ESP test encouraging competition. It was hypothesized that within each pair one would consistently score positively and the other negatively. The experimenter would be able to predict from behavior which would score in which direction. Three series (80 runs) resulted in significant differences in scoring between predicted positive and negative students ($p < .0001$).

57. Krippner, S. (1965). **Coding and clairvoyance in a dual aspect test with children.** *Perceptual and Motor Skills*, *20*, 745-748.

Thirty-seven boys and three girls (ages 8-16) were given two series of clairvoyance tests. The first contained 25 cards, with five photographs each of dogs, cats, fish, boats, and ships. The second series had 25 cards with five each of the words dogs, cats, fish, boats, and ships. Test I showed nonsignificant results, while test II was significant ($p = .01$), with students scoring better on word than on picture targets. The overall total number of hits was significant ($p = .01$).

58. Moriarity, A. E. & Murphy, G. (1967). **Some thoughts about the prerequisite conditions or states in creativity and paranormal experiences.** *Journal of the American Society for Psychical Research*, *61*, 203-218.

Fifty-seven adolescents were assessed by a ten-point creativity scale, then later tested for ESP. (See next listing for experimental results.) The article describes five variables considered as important aspects for creativity: 1) openness to external world; 2) openness to internal world; 3) capacity for dissociability; 4) capacity for structuring; 5) capacity for communication.

59. Moriarity, A. E. & Murphy, G. (1967). **An experimental study of ESP potential and its relationship to creativity in a group of normal children.** Journal of the American Society for Psychical Research, 61, 326-338.

Forty-two adolescent subjects were tested for ESP after having been rated for creativity (see listing above by same authors). Results showed nonsignificant ESP expression with some consistent trends toward ESP and creativity.

60. Peretti, P. O. & Gierkey, J. (1978). **Clairvoyance performance in youth.** Journal of Psychological Researches, 22, 21-32.

Clairvoyance testing was conducted individually using Zener cards on 163 children (ages 4-18). There were seven equal groups for age and sex, with three runs for a total of 75 trials. Significant results were found for girls in the 6.1- to 8-year, 8.1- to 10-year, and 12.1- to 14-year groups. Significance levels and statistical methods used were not reported.

61. Pratt, J. G. & Price, M. M. (1937). **The experimenter-subject relationship in tests for ESP.** Journal of Parapsychology, 2, 84-94.

Two series of ESP experiments were conducted with children (ages 8-16). Section I entailed treating some of the 40 subjects "favorably" and others "unfavorably," to see if the experimenter's behavior affected ESP scores. Chance results were obtained. In Section II, the experimenter adopted a previously successful approach toward subjects and obtained significant scores, concluding that experimenter behavior affects subjects' performance on ESP tasks.

62. Price, M. M. (1938). **A comparison of blind and seeing subjects in ESP tests.** Journal of Parapsychology, 2, 273-286.

A group of 66 blind boys (ages 8-23) were compared with a group of 40 seeing subjects (ages 8-16) for ESP test performance over 52,975 trials. Results as a whole were highly significant, with blind subjects showing fairly consistently higher average scores than nonblind subjects. A quarter of the runs were conducted with sealed opaque envelopes containing the targets, and in both groups these gave significantly higher results than runs using open cards.

63. Price, M. M. & Pegram, M. H. (1937). **Extra-sensory perception among the blind.** Journal of Parapsychology, 1, 143-155.

Sixty-six blind subjects, ranging in age from 8 to 35, were given various card-calling tests. Results were statistically significant. When subjects matched sealed cards, their scores were higher than in similar matching of open cards. Of 28 subjects ages 11 to 15, 54% gave individually significant scores; of 22 subjects ages 16 to 20, 41% gave individually significant scores; and of 9 subjects ages 21 to 35, 33% gave individually significant scores.

64. Randall, J. L. (1972). **Group ESP experiments with schoolboys.** Journal of Parapsychology, 36, 133-143. (Reprinted as **Experimentos de ESP con un grupo de escolares.** Cuadernos de Parapsicologia, 1972, 5, 1-11.)

An ESP pilot study with 29 grammar-school boys (age 14) completed two telepathy runs with a teacher as sender and clairvoyance runs using ESP cards as targets. As a whole, the group did not score significantly above chance on either task. A positive correlation ($p < .03$) between telepathy and clairvoyance scores was found. Results of a questionnaire given indicated eight significant scorers suffered from hay fever. A significantly high subject variance was found on the Junior Eysenck Personality Inventory for the high neurotic and high extrovert scorers. A second experiment with 31 subjects yielded similar results to the pilot. Overall scoring was nonsignificant, but subject variance was significant as was the correlation between ESP and clairvoyance. Hay fever sufferers again scored above chance, and high extrovert, high neurotic subjects showed high subject variance.

65. Sailaja, P. & Rao, P. V. (1978). **Response patterns and psi scoring.** Journal of Parapsychology, 42, 304-312.

Two series of studies, using 50 female subjects (ages 12-14) and 49 subjects (ages 10-12), attempted to replicate findings by Kanthamani and Rao (1975). The numbers of meaningful words subjects checked as ESP responses over alternative meaningless words was felt to be a good predictor of how well subjects would do on the clairvoyance part of the test. In the first series, there was significant correlation ($p < .01$) between the number of meaningful words checked and ESP scores obtained. The results of the second series were nonsignificant. Nonsignificant results overall were found between the first and second series on relationship between ESP scores and subjects' expectation of success.

66. Schmeidler, G. R. (1962). **ESP and tests of perception.** Journal of the American Society for Psychical Research, 56, 48-51.

One personality test, two perception tests, and an ESP test were given to 30 children in a cottage-type orphanage and 19 children living at home. IQ scores were available for 23 orphanage children. The average age was 11 years. Results showed significant positive correlation of ESP scores with speed of finding hidden pictures and a suggestive positive correlation between ESP and IQ.

67. Schmeidler, G. R. (1971). **Mood and attitude on a pretest as predictors of retest ESP performance.** Journal of the American Society for Psychical Research, 65, 324-343.

A pilot with 20 interested college students showed a high correlation between ESP scores and a combination of mood scores. A follow-up study with 51 eagerly interested junior high schoolers indicated that when mood and attitude shifted, ESP scores shifted predictably.

68. Targ, R. A. & Cole, P. (1975). **Use of an automatic stimulus generator to teach ESP** [Summary]. In J. D. Morris, W. G. Roll, & R. L. Morris (Eds.), Research in Parapsychology 1974, (pp. 27-29). Metuchen, NJ: Scarecrow Press.

Out of 145 subjects, 66 were children (ages 12-14), and the remainder were adults. Each person was repeatedly tested for clairvoyant learning on a four-choice, random stimulus generator, using 35mm color slides of paintings as targets. Subjects had the choice of whether or not to respond on each trial. Through a screening of the subjects, six subjects were found to have significantly improved their scoring ($p = .01$). Additional subjects had significantly high mean scores over the total two testing periods (1400-2800 trials). Also discussed is additional testing that was done with smaller groups of subjects showing ability.

69. Weisinger, C. (1971). **Clairvoyant experiments with school children.** *Journal of Parapsychology*, *35*, 62-63.

A total of 451 students (ages 7-15), were individually given two clairvoyance tests, the first using five different pictures as targets and the second using five different clock positions. The targets were placed in the desk of a best friend without the knowledge of the subject. Overall results were significant ($p = .0018$), while clock positions targets yielded nonsignificant scores.

70. Weisinger, C. (1973). **Two ESP experiments in the classroom.** *Journal of Parapsychology*, *37*, 76-77.

A total of 325 German and Swiss boys (ages 8-15) had to guess the numbers 0 to 9 as targets for two runs, with their teacher as telepathic agent. Overall results were nonsignificant, with no correlation found between ESP and the child's attitude toward the teacher, or the teacher-child attitude. The teacher's attitude toward parapsychology significantly correlated with the ESP score of the class ($p = .01$). Two additional experiments with children as agents were significant ($p < .0004$, $p < .009$). A reanalysis of data found significant results of spontaneous psi communication among children. Children tended to take psi information from the most popular classmates ($p < .005$).

In a second series, 451 boys (ages 7-15) were given a clairvoyance card task. Each subject thought he was guessing a down-through deck of 25 cards, when the deck actually contained blank cards. The real targets were unknown to the subject, in close proximity to a popular classmate. Results were significant ($p = .0032$).

71. Winkelman, M. (1981). **The effect of formal education on extrasensory abilities: The Ozolco Study.** *Journal of Parapsychology*, *45*, 321-336.

Three experiments assessed whether or not an increase in formal education inhibits ESP abilities. Subjects were 29 children from a rural Mexican village (ages 8-14) with 0 to 7 years of education. Clairvoyance testing with candy yielded significant results ($p < .005$), while use of marbles in clairvoyant testing was nonsignificant. Precognitive testing with candy was significant at the .05 level, while precognition using marbles was nonsignificant. PK testing using marbles yielded $p < .1$. There were no strong significant differences between males and females. Additional testing of field independence, conservation, math, and years of schooling were correlated. Total ESP correlated negatively with math ($p < .02$), schooling ($p < .03$), conservation, field independence, and age. Similar negative correlations were found with clairvoyance and precognition testing. PK correlated positively with age ($p < .006$).

C. High schoolers (15-17 years)

72. Anderson, M. L. (1959). **The relationship between level of ESP scoring and student class grade.** Journal of Parapsychology, 23, 1-18.

The article examines 10 research studies carried out with 1,228 students at nine different grade levels (fifth through junior college, the majority high schoolers). A statistically significant relationship was found between ESP scores and grades; students who received high grades (A and B) tended to average above chance on ESP tests, while students with lower grades (D and E) scored below chance. The C students did not show ESP. Teacher-pupil attitudes were also analyzed, with the most striking negative ESP deviation by the D and E students who disliked their teachers. Those D and E students with a favorable teacher attitude scored close to chance.

73. Anderson, M. L. & White, R. A. (1956). **Teacher-pupil attitudes and clairvoyance test results.** Journal of Parapsychology, 20, 141-157.

The article reviews clairvoyance experiments with seven high school classes (grades 9-12) in five different states, with a total of 28,500 ESP trials by 228 students. Teachers and pupils also filled out questionnaires designed to reveal attitudes toward each other. Overall results of the clairvoyant tests were nonsignificant. However, when ESP results were broken down according to the teacher's attitude toward the student, significant positive scoring was related to positive attitudes. Nonsignificant negative scoring was associated with negative attitudes, and a significant difference was found between the two groups. Additional significant results in teacher-pupil attitudes are discussed.

74. Anderson, M. L. & White, R. A. (1957). **A further investigation of teacher and pupil attitudes and clairvoyance test results.** Journal of Parapsychology, 21, 81-97.

Teachers administered ESP tests, consisting of a list of randomized ESP symbols, to 205 high schoolers (grades 9-12). A total of 25,625 trials were conducted. Students also filled out questionnaires on how they liked their teacher, and teachers rated students. Scoring trends indicated that when pupils were liked by the teacher, they scored significantly above chance, while those students who were disliked scored insignificantly. The difference between the two groups was significant. Additional analyses are discussed.

75. Anderson, M. L. & White, R. A. (1958). **A survey of work on ESP and teacher-pupil attitudes.** Journal of Parapsychology, 22, 246-268.

The article reviews nine exploratory studies with high schoolers on teacher-pupil attitudes and levels of ESP scoring, carried out in 1957 to 1958. Though some of the results were similar to earlier findings, scoring differences did not reach levels of significance. The authors also give a complete summary of work to date on the relationship of ESP scoring to teacher-pupil attitudes.

NOTE: Van de Castle, R. L. (1959). **A review of ESP tests carried out in the classroom.** International Journal of Parapsychology, 1, 84-102. Also Murphy, G. & Anderson, M. L. (1959). **Experimental objectives of the Anderson-White work with school children.** Journal of Parapsychology, 23, 133-135. Both articles review and analyze studies conducted by Anderson & White. For a brief description of these articles, see listing: Telepathy, Pre-School/Elementary.

76. Deguisne, A. (1959). **Two repetitions of the Anderson-White investigation of teacher-pupil attitudes and clairvoyance test results. Part I: High school tests.** Journal of Parapsychology, 23, 196-207.

Subjects were 185 high schoolers from seven classes who were given sealed envelopes containing a list of ESP symbols and asked to fill out a questionnaire rating their teachers. Teachers also rated the students. Results were in the direction found by Anderson and White. When student and teacher liked each other, the student scored in a positive direction. When there was a mutual dislike, the scores were negative. On this experiment, students who liked their teacher scored significantly higher than those students who disliked their teacher. (See Goldstone, G. **Two repetitions of the Anderson-White investigation of teacher-pupil attitudes and clairvoyance test results. Part II: Grade-school tests.** Journal of Parapsychology, 1959, 23, 208-213, Pre-School/-Elementary Clairvoyance listing.)

77. Eason, M. J. C. & Wysocki, B. A. (1965). **Extrasensory perception and intelligence.** Journal of Parapsychology, 29, 109-114.

A total of 98 freshmen and sophomore high school girls (ages 13-16) were separated into one group with IQs 90 to 110 and another with IQs 125 to 144. After one ESP trial, results showed no relationship between intelligence and ESP. When scores of both groups were combined, there was significant evidence of ESP ($p < .002$).

78. Feather, S. R. (1967). **A quantitative comparison of memory and psi.** Journal of Parapsychology, 31, 93-98.

A clairvoyance test with ESP symbols was given first to 30 high schoolers, followed by memorization of 25 ESP symbols within a 15-second interval. Subjects were then given additional ESP trials. Finally, subjects were asked to recall as many of the previously memorized targets as possible. Overall results of the three series showed a significantly positive correlation ($p = .01$) between ESP and memory scores.

79. Foster, E. B. (1956). **A re-examination of Dr. Soal's "clairvoyance" data.** Journal of Parapsychology, 20, 110-120.

The author questions whether Soal, in his GESP investigation of a Spanish girl, might not have overlooked indications of clairvoyance. The author notes that Langdon-Davies obtained results that were as high for clairvoyance as for GESP. However, Soal and Bateman's work yielded only chance results with clairvoyance and significantly positive evidence with GESP. The author questions whether Soal and his associates may have introduced some psychological factor that allows the operation of ESP under GESP conditions but inhibits its function under conditions allowing only clairvoyance to occur. (See listing this section: Langdon-Davies, J., Bateman, F., and Soal, S. G., 1955.)

80. Gambale, J. (1976). **Word frequency and associative strength in memory-ESP interaction: A failure to replicate.** Journal of Parapsychology, 40, 339-340.

Fifty high school juniors and seniors (26 females, 24 males) studied 20 paired items, one of which was a trigram and the other a word (half were highly-associative, the other half not). Subjects were then required to list the missing word for each pair and circle which one of the pair was preselected as the ESP target. Overall results were nonsignificant. A statistically significant post hoc analysis is discussed.

81. Giesler, P. V. (1985). **An attempted replication of Winkelman's ESP and socialization research** [Summary]. In R. White & J. Solfvin (Eds.), Research in Parapsychology 1984 (pp. 24-27). Metuchen, NJ: Scarecrow Press.

Thirty-six children living in Brazil (ages 8-16; 18 males, 18 females), were given 30 trials of a clairvoyance (CV) task, 40 PK trials, and a formal math test with educational years controlled. The CV test involved guessing which of three colored candy balls out of nine total would be selected; the reward given was a similar candy from a different bag. The PK task required influencing a random-event generator to light either one of two light bulbs on its machine, with one series having a small statue of a regional deity behind one bulb. Overall PK and CV scores were negative and nonsignificant, thus not confirming Winkelman's results. CV, PK, and math correlations were nonsignificant.

82. Haight, J. M. (1979). **Spontaneous psi cases: A survey and preliminary study of ESP, attitude and personality relationships.** Journal of Parapsychology, 43, 179-204.

Subjects were several groupings totaling 254 high school students (ages 15-19), of whom 112 reported psi-related experience. They were given the High School Personality Questionnaire, clairvoyance tests, and an attitude and experience questionnaire. Subjects reporting psi experiences scored significantly higher than non-psi subjects ($p < .05$), due to the non-psi subjects' psi-missing.

83. Harary, S. B. (1976). **A study of psi, memory, and expectancy** [Summary]. In J. D. Morris, W. G. Roll, & R. L. Morris (Eds.), Research in Parapsychology 1975 (pp. 121-126). Metuchen, NJ: Scarecrow Press.

Two groups of high schoolers memorized lists of paired-associates that were hard, with another two groups memorizing an easier list. They were then given sealed envelopes with another list containing only half of the paired-associates pasted to the front. Students had to enter the missing associates in one of the two blank spaces next to each word. The number of recall-correct responses was significantly lower in the more difficult memorization task. Nonsignificant psi results were obtained. Additional analyses are discussed and possible explanations for results offered.

84. Johnson, M. & Kanthamani, B. K. (1967). **The Defense Mechanism Test as a predictor of ESP scoring direction.** Journal of Parapsychology, 31, 99-110.

Using the Defense Mechanism Test to measure anxiety tolerance, the relationship between ESP and anxiety was investigated with paid high school subjects. Subjects were tested in pairs for ESP on a competitive clairvoyance procedure. A pilot study with 16 students showed a significant correlation ($p < .005$) with high-defense raters psi missing and low-defense raters psi hitters. A second confirmatory study with 11 students also was significant ($p < .05$).

85. Jones, J. N. & Feather, S. R. (1969). **Relationship between reports of psi experiences and subject variance.** Journal of Parapsychology, 33, 311-319.

Groups of junior high and high school subjects, after listening to a talk on ESP, filled out a five-item psi experience questionnaire and took an ESP test. Two preliminary series (51 high schoolers) and a pilot study showed nonsignificant results. A post hoc analysis indicated that subjects with the greater number of ESP experiences had a greater variance in scoring than did those who had fewer experiences. A first confirmatory series (53 high schoolers) gave results that were in the same direction ($p < .025$). A second confirmatory series (275 junior high schoolers) was at chance level. The difference between the two series gave suggestive results ($p < .05$).

86. Kanthamani, B. K. & Rao, K. R. (1971). **Personality characteristics of ESP subjects: I. Primary personality characteristics and ESP.** Journal of Parapsychology, 35, 189-207.

A pilot and three confirmatory studies were conducted on the relationship between personality characteristics and ESP among 146 male and female Indian students (ages 16-18). ESP card runs and Cattell's High School Personality Questionnaire were administered. Subjects rated as warm and sociable scored higher on the ESP task than did those rated as critical and aloof. Those rated as dominant scored positively, and those rated as submissive scored negatively. "Happy-go-lucky" subjects scored positively, while "serious-minded" subjects scored negatively. "Touch and realistic" subjects scored higher than the aesthetically sensitive ones on ESP tests. The difference between each of the groups was statistically significant.

87. Kanthamani, B. K. & Rao, K. R. (1972). **Personality characteristics of ESP subjects: II. The combined personality measure (CPM) and ESP.** Journal of Parapsychology, 36, 56-70.

A total of 146 high schoolers were measured for various personality characteristics (reserved vs. outgoing, humble vs. assertive, sober vs. happy-go-lucky, tough-minded vs. tender-minded) and were divided into high- and low-CPM scorers and then tested for ESP. Analysis of the series indicated that high-CPM subjects obtained more hits than low-CPM subjects. The difference between the groups was statistically significant. The results of three confirmatory experiments supported these findings. The combined results were significant ($p < .001$).

88. Kanthamani, B. K. & Rao, K. R. (1972). **Personality characteristics of ESP subjects: III. Extraversion and ESP.** Journal of Parapsychology, 36, 198-212.

This study examined the relationship between ESP and extraversion in 146 Indian high schoolers. Subjects completed an ESP test and a personality questionnaire. In the pilot study, extraverts scored above chance while introverts scored below chance on the ESP task ($p < .01$). All three replications yielded similar results. The combined results were highly significant ($p < .00005$).

89. Kanthamani, B. K. & Rao, K. R. (1973). **Personality characteristics of ESP subjects: IV. Neuroticism and ESP.** Journal of Parapsychology, 37, 37-50.

The relationship between neuroticism (N) scores and ESP scores of 146 high schoolers were studied. A pilot and three confirmatory studies showed low-N students obtained more ESP hits than high-N students. The difference between the two groups was significant ($p = .001$). Additional analyses of the individual factors of the N-scale are discussed.

90. Kanthamani, B. K. & Rao, K. R. (1973). **Personality characteristics of ESP subjects: V. Graphic expansiveness and ESP.** Journal of Parapsychology, 37, 119-129.

A clairvoyance test, a drawing test of expansiveness-compressiveness, and the extroversion scale from the High School Personality Questionnaire were administered to 110 female high school and junior college students. Expansive students scored significantly higher on ESP tasks than compressive students ($p < .05$). The difference in scoring rate was highly significant ($p < .001$).

91. Kanthamani, H. & Rao, H. H. (1974). **A study of memory-ESP relationships using linguistic forms.** Journal of Parapsychology, 38, 286-300.

A total of 62 high schoolers had to learn a list of word-pairs, later recall them, and then choose which of the two words was the ESP target. A total of four series were conducted. Results of the pilot (16 subjects) and two confirmatory studies (20 subjects in each) showed correctly recalled trials yielded significant ESP scores. Combined results of the two confirmatory series yielded highly significant ($p < .005$) scores for recall-correct trials, insignificant scores for recall-wrong trials. The overall difference between the two categories was significant ($p < .025$).

92. Kanthamani, H. & Rao, H. H. (1975). **The role of association strength in memory-ESP interaction.** Journal of Parapsychology, 39, 1-11.

Two series of 20 word-pairs (one set with strong associations between words and the other with weak associations) were given to 20 high schoolers to memorize within a short time. They then filled in the missing word within the pair on one of two blank spaces. The results confirmed psi-hitting where recall was correct and psi-missing on items where recall was wrong. The difference between the groups was significant ($p < .05$) in both series and with pooled data.

93. Krishna, S. R. & Rao, K. R. (1981). **Personality and "belief" in relation to language ESP scores** [Summary]. In W. G. Roll & J. Beloff (Eds.), Research in Parapsychology 1980 (pp. 61-63). Metuchen, NJ: Scarecrow Press.

Three different clairvoyance tests involving Telugu and English target words were given to 95 high school subjects. Personality scores were also obtained and correlated with ESP scores. In the pilot study, emotional stability and warm-hearted, easygoing, and outgoing characteristics were significantly and positively correlated with ESP. The confirmatory series showed a nonsignificant similar trend. Nonsignificant ESP scores were obtained between sheep and goats. Only dual- and single-target conditions yielded significant results for the sheep group ($p < .05$).

94. Langdon-Davies, J. L., Bateman, F., & Soal, S. G. (1955). **ESP tests with a Spanish girl.** Journal of Parapsychology, 19, 155-163.

High scoring ESP ability in Maria, a 16-year-old Spanish kitchen maid, was tested under informal exploratory conditions. In both tests of clairvoyance and GESP, above-chance scores were obtained by Langdon-Davies. However, clairvoyance scores dropped to chance under the testing conducted by Soal and Bateman. Maria continued to score above chance on GESP tests with Soal and Bateman. (See additional listing, this section: E. B. Foster, 1956, regarding this experiment.)

95. Langdon-Davies, J. L. (1956). **Extrasensory perception among peasant European populations.** In Wolstenholme, G. E. W. & Millar, E. C. P. (Eds.), Extrasensory perception: A Ciba Foundation symposium, (pp. 111-119). NY: Citadel Press.

Several series of ESP card tests were conducted with Maria, a 16-year-old Spanish girl, under a variety of conditions. The first tests used as agents other servants in the Langdon-Davies household, whereas later (clairvoyance) tests involved Maria alone. As changes were introduced into the testing procedure, Maria's scores would fall, then gradually rise again. Maria scored well above chance, but after some 20,000 trials, decline began to set in. A later experiment with F. Bateman as agent was again highly significant. The combined Langdon-Davies and Bateman experiments gave results with odds of 26 million to 1 against chance expectation.

96. Munson, R. J. (1981). **Belief and sex difference in a language differential test** [Summary]. In W. G. Roll & J. Beloff (Eds.), Research in Parapsychology 1980 (pp. 63-64). Metuchen, NJ: Scarecrow Press.

A clairvoyance experiment was conducted with 49 college students (pilot study) and 129 high school students, using English and Telugu word sheets randomly selected by computer. Subjects were divided into sheep and goat groups. The pilot study showed overall nonsignificant results, with goats scoring significantly negatively against chance ($p < .02$). The remaining tests with high school subjects were overall nonsignificant, with some suggestive effects in male sheep groupings.

97. Murray, D. M. (1983). **The effect of schooling on the manifestation of clairvoyant abilities among Isnag children of the Northern Philippines** [Summary]. In W. G. Roll, J. Beloff, & R. White (Eds.), Research in Parapsychology 1982 (pp. 245-248). Metuchen, NJ: Scarecrow Press.

Subjects were 36 children, ages 8-16 years, four children per category. The clairvoyance test consisted of 30 three-target trials using 60 red, yellow, and green candies. A math skills test was also administered. T-test results were nonsignificant for clairvoyance. Multiple regression analysis results indicated that males had statistically higher clairvoyance scores than females ($p < .05$). This study failed to replicate Winkelman's (1981) study showing significant negative correlations between age and clairvoyance.

98. Nielsen, W. & Freeman, J. (1965). **Consistency of relationships between ESP and emotional variables.** Journal of Parapsychology, 29, 75-88.

High schoolers (217) and college students (36) were given ESP tasks from one or more of two-word tests, tests using standard ESP symbols, and psychological tests. Results showed high-anxious subjects had higher overall ESP scores than mid- and low-anxious subjects.

99. O'Brien, J. L. T. & O'Brien, D. P. (1977). **Psi in the classroom: A replication and extension** [Summary]. In J. D. Morris, W. G. Roll, & R. L. Morris (Eds.), Research in Parapsychology 1976 (pp. 140-142). Metuchen, NJ: Scarecrow Press.

A high school teacher gave an ESP test to 133 students in five parapsychology classes. The examination had 30 multiple choice questions with 15 "real" answers in the students' books and 15 "made up" ones. Of the five classes, three showed predicted hitter/misser scoring trends, and two showed insignificant reversals.

100. Palmer, J., Ader, C., & Mikova, M. (1981). **Anxiety and ESP: Anatomy of a reversal** [Summary]. In W. G. Roll & J. Beloff (Eds.), Research in Parapsychology 1980 (pp. 77-81). Metuchen, NJ: Scarecrow Press.

High school students (40) were rated on an anxiety scale and randomly assigned to one of four experimental groups. The conditions were: 1) immediate feedback on both four-run blocks (F/F), 2) no feedback until end of blocks (N/N), 3) immediate feedback on first block (F/N), and 4) feedback on last block only (N/F). Testing was conducted on a 4-choice ESP tester with internal electronic RNG. Results were nonsignificant. When comfort in the test was assessed, the results were that 29 subjects with a positive rating scored significantly above the remaining subjects ($p < .05$). A follow-up experiment with 40 high school subjects showed that anxiety-ESP correlation was nonsignificant, but it did reach significance for the first block separately ($p = .05$).

101. Peretti, P. O. & Gierkey, J. (1978). **Clairvoyance performance in youth.** Journal of Psychological Researches, 22, 21-32.

Clairvoyance testing was conducted individually, using Zener cards on 163 children (ages 4-18); there were seven groups equal for age and sex. With three runs for a total of 75 trials, significant results were found for girls in the 6.1- to 8-year, 8.1- to 10-year, and 12.1- to 14-year groups. Significance levels and statistical methods used were not reported.

102. Rammohan, V. G. & Rao, P. V. K. (1987). **ESP performance in classroom examination settings.** Journal of Indian Psychology, 6, 24-37.

A clairvoyance study was conducted using test booklets with real and made-up (ESP) questions, with multiple choice answers. College and high school students (683, ages 16-20) were used. Results were nonsignificant, indicating that ESP performance did not differ across situations or with subject attitude.

103. Randall, J. L. (1974). **Card-guessing experiments with school boys.** Journal of the Society for Psychical Research, 47, 421-432. (Reprinted in abstract form in Journal of Parapsychology, 1975, 39, 90-91.)

Results of six classroom experiments with 169 high school boys yielded 16 students obtaining ESP scores that were marginally significant ($p < .05$) and six scoring highly significantly ($p < .01$). There was a general tendency for scores obtained under clairvoyance to be marginally positively correlated ($p = .04$) with scores under GESP conditions. Additionally, students classified as both high- extrovert and high-neurotic on the Junior Eysenck Personality Scale showed high subject variance ($p = .0008$). Subjects classified as both low-extrovert and low-neurotic also obtained significant subject variance ($p = .02$).

104. Rao, K. R. (1965). **ESP and The Manifest Anxiety Scale.** Journal of Parapsychology, 29, 12-18.

A group of 57 high schoolers were divided into high-anxious and low-anxious groups.. The high-anxious group scored below chance on an ESP task, while the low-anxious group scored above, giving a significant difference between groups ($p = .01$).

105. Rao, K. R., Morrison, M., & Davis, J. W. (1978). **Paired-associates recall and ESP: A study of memory and psi-missing** [Summary]. In W. G. Roll (Ed.), Research in Parapsychology 1977 (pp. 65-84). Metuchen, NJ: Scarecrow Press.

A paired-associate learning sheet (nonsense syllables) was given to 150 high schoolers, along with an ESP-recall sheet to test for intentional and unintentional psi. Overall ESP scores were nonsignificant.

106. Rao, K. R. (1978). **Further studies of memory and ESP.** Journal of Parapsychology, 42, 167-178.

This reports the third in a series of experiments exploring memory and ESP, through paired memorization of nonsense trigrams with meaningful words. Intermixed with the familiar words were new ESP target words. Ninety-five subjects ranging from high school and college ages to senior citizens volunteered. The research does not break down results by age. Overall results were nonsignificant for memory and ESP scores. However, Group I showed a tendency ($p < .05$) for "hitters" to respond with the words ranked more closely associated with targets. The "missers" did the opposite.

107. Rao, K. R. & Kanthamani, H. (1981). **Possible sex-related differences of same and opposite sex pairs in competition/cooperation experiments.** Journal of Indian Psychology, 3, 41-51.

Three series of clairvoyance tests were given using 60 subject-pairs of high school students. Subject-pairs were in competing and cooperative situations, using same and different Zener card targets. Results were nonsignificant. A post-hoc analysis revealed significant sex differences.

108. Rao, K. R., Kanthamani, H., & Norwood, B. (1983). **Sex-related differential scoring in two volitional studies.** Journal of Parapsychology, 47, 7-21.

Forty same- and twenty opposite-sex pairs of high school students were given a clairvoyance task, under conditions of competition and cooperation. Results were nonsignificant in terms of showing that scores of competing pairs would be higher than those of the cooperative pairs. A post-hoc analysis yielded significant sex-related differences in scoring. A follow-up study with 42 pairs of subjects showed that male vs. female ESP scores differed significantly ($p < .05$), and these differences tended to be significantly larger than with same-sex pairs.

109. Rao, K. R., Morrison, M., & Davis, J. W. (1977). **Paired-associates recall and ESP: A study of memory and psi-missing.** Journal of Parapsychology, 41, 165-189.

Six high school classes and one college class had to memorize a list of paired associates containing one nonsense trigram and one of 10 meaningful words. They then had to recall the associated word when presented with the trigram. Intermixed with familiar trigrams were new nonsense syllables whose correct associates could be known only through ESP. Subjects ranked each of 10 meaningful words as to how closely associated they felt them to be. Results showed significant difference ($p < .02$) between mean association rank scores of hitters and missers. A second replication study with 118 high school subjects yielded nonsignificant results in the predicted direction.

110. Rao, K. R. & Norwood, B. (1983). **An attempted replication of sex differences in volitional studies** [Summary]. In W. G. Roll, J. Beloff, and R. A. White (Eds.), Research in Parapsychology 1982 (pp. 200-201). Metuchen, NJ: Scarecrow Press.

A clairvoyance experiment used 42 pairs of high school students under cooperative and competitive conditions. Computer-generated ESP symbols and concealed target sheets were used. Scores of opposite-sex pairs were significant in the competition condition ($p < .05$) vs. the scores of the competing subjects of same-sex pairs. Data analysis to test for the volitional effect was nonsignificant (chance level).

111. Rilling, M. E., Pettijohn, C., & Adams, J. Q. (1961). **A two-experimenter investigation of teacher-pupil attitudes and clairvoyance test results in the high school classsroom.** Journal of Parapsychology, 25, 247-259.

An attempt to replicate the Anderson-White experiments on teacher-pupil attitudes was conducted with 16 high schoolers. Overall results were nonsignificant and failed to replicate the previous study.

112. Rivers, O. B. (1950). **An exploratory study of the mental health and intelligence of ESP subjects.** Journal of Parapsychology, 14, 267-277.

Two groups of 36 college men and 36 high school boys were given a series of clairvoyance and GESP tests, as well as a mental health analysis. While total ESP scores were statistically significant, the mental health analysis did not prove reliable in selecting good ESP subjects.

113. Stanford, R. G. (1967). **Response bias and the correctness of ESP test responses.** Journal of Parapsychology, 31, 280-289.

Twenty-eight high schoolers were given the task of locating "targets" on a mock "radar screen" containing 36 sections. The screens containing the actual targets were in an opaque sealed envelope held up by the subject. Subjects giving a low frequency of calls had significantly more hits ($p <$ .0005) than the high-frequency callers ($p < .06$). The difference between the groups was significant ($p \cong .00005$).

114. Van de Castle, R. L. & White, R. A. (1955). **A report on a sentence completion form of sheep-goat attitude scale.** Journal of Parapsychology, 19, 171-179.

An ESP test was conducted in two group settings with each of the 39 high school students presented with an individual target series (sealed in an opaque envelope). One session of four clairvoyance runs, followed by a talk by the experimenter, followed by four additional ESP runs were given. Subjects' attitudes toward ESP were obtained in advance of the testing. The 18 "sheep" subjects' average score was above expectation and the 10 "goat" subjects' average score was below expectation. Eleven subjects rated as having conflict over the existence of ESP averaged at a level between the other two groups. None of the three groups gave significant results.

115. White, R. A. & Angstadt, J. (1961). **A resume of research at the ASPR into teacher-pupil attitudes and clairvoyance test results, 1959-1960.** Journal of the American Society for Psychical Research, 55, 142-147.

An attempted replication of the Anderson-White experiment, of teacher-pupil attitudes and a clairvoyance test, involved 18 teachers and 471 high schoolers. Results were nonsignificant and yielded a failure to replicate.

II. TELEPATHY

II. TELEPATHY

A. Pre-school/elementary age (infancy to 12 years)

116. Bender, H. (1938). **The case of Ilga K.: Report of a phenomenon of unusual perception.** Journal of Parapsychology, 2, 5-22.

This reports on a 1935 case of Professor Neureiter, of a mentally retarded ten-year-old Latvian girl who appeared to be able to "read thoughts." She was able to "read" any text, even in a language foreign to her, if Prof. Neureiter stood beside her silently reading the text. Three studies of the child were made, each concluding that she had ESP. The German commission made movie and dictaphone records of the experiments and concluded that most of her responses were explainable in terms of acute auditory ability, while also acknowledging a number of conversations that could not be explained by this theory.

117. Berger, R. E. (1989). **Discussion: A critical examination of the Blackmore psi experiments.** Journal of the American Society for Psychical Research, 83, 123-144.

Blackmore's psi experiment data base (two experiments conducted with young children) is examined and found to have discrepancies between unpublished reports and published counterparts. Blackmore's claims that her data base shows no evidence of psi are called unfounded. Berger states that no conclusions at all can be drawn from her data base.

Blackmore, S. J. **A critical response to Rick Berger**, 145-154.

Blackmore finds Berger's accusations unfounded; where she failed to replicate Spinelli's results with children, she traces the problem to Spinelli's reportage and statistics.

Berger, R. E. **Reply to Blackmore's "A critical response to Rick Berger."** 155-157. Berger refutes points made by Blackmore.

118. Berger, R.E. (1989). **A critical examination of the Spinelli data.** Journal of the Society for Psychical Research, 56, 28-34.

In examining Spinelli's ESP experiments with children, Berger finds unexplained statistical anomalies and errors which lead him to question Spinelli's findings that younger children get better psi results than older ones or adults do. Berger hypothesizes that because children require different handling than adults do, Spinelli's special treatment of the children may have led to the artifact(s) which (mis)led Spinelli to conclude that especially young children show extraordinary levels of psi. (See Spinelli, E.: 1977, 1983, 1984, 1987.)

Spinelli, E. **A reply to Dr. Berger's note,** 34-38. Spinelli does not know what these artifact(s) might have been. Until his studies are replicated, however, he does not think that his research work can constitute conclusive evidence,

119. Blackmore, S. (1980). **A study of memory and ESP in young children.** Journal of the Society for Psychical Research, 50, 501-520.

The literature on ESP in children is reviewed and found to show little systemic evidence of a relationship between ESP and age. In a pilot study, 19 playgroup children (ages 3-6) were tested for clairvoyance and GESP, with different colored candies as targets. Results were not significant. In the main experiment, subjects were 48 children from three playgroups (ages 3-5). Children were given memory and preference tests. Targets were colored pictures on white cards. Children took turns as sender and receiver. Results showed no significant correlation of either memory or age of the child with ESP.

120. Blackmore, S. (1984). **ESP in young children: A critique on the Spinelli evidence.** Journal of the Society for Psychical Research, 52, 311-315. (See also Spinelli, 1987; Spinelli, 1983.)

The article critizes Spinelli's theory of GESP abilities as inverse to development, which is based on his research where the youngest subjects scored highest. The artifact of sender choice is felt to account for these results.

121. Bond, E. M. (1937). **General extrasensory perception with a group of fourth and fifth grade children.** Journal of Parapsychology, 1, 114-122.

A class of 22 retarded children (ages 9-14) guessed numbers that the teacher concentrated on. The group scored significantly above chance. Four of the children made individually significant scores. No reliable correlation was found between scoring ability and intelligence rating.

122. Burlingham, D. T. (1935). **Child analysis and the mother.** Psychoanalytic Quarterly, 5, 69-92.

The author cites several instances of "certain striking parallelisms between the thought or behavior of the mother and that of the children, which do not seem understandable in terms of familiar forms of communication between mother and child."

123. Burt, C. (1959). **Experiments on telepathy in children: Critical notice.** British Journal of Statistical Psychology, 12, 55-99.

This describes and defends in detail research conducted by S. G. Soal and H. T. Bowden, as described in their book The Mind Readers. Two 13-year-old boys showed telepathic and clairvoyant ability on card tests. The author refutes at length Hansel's arguments against the possibility of ESP occurring. A section is devoted to conditions best suited for ESP success, applicable to tests with both adults and children. Hypotheses to be investigated for a better understanding of the nature of ESP are also listed. (See additional listings, this section: Burt, 1960; Hansel, 1960; Nicol, 1960; Thouless, 1961; and Book Reviews.)

124. Burt, C. (1960). **Experiments on telepathy in children: A reply to Mr. Hansel's criticisms.** British Journal of Statistical Psychology, 13, 179-188.

This is a continuing discussion on research conducted by S. G. Soal and H. T. Bowden on the supposedly telepathic and clairvoyant Jones boys. (See additional listings this section: Burt, 1959; Hansel, 1960; Nicol, 1960; Thouless, 1961, and Book Reviews.

125. Drewes, A. A. & Drucker, S. A. (1977). **The effects of mother-child telepathy on a visual-perception task** [Summary]. In J. D. Morris, W. G. Roll, & R. L. Morris (Eds.), Research in Parapsychology 1976 (pp. 100-102). Metuchen, NJ: Scarecrow Press.

Twenty children (ages 5-9) were grouped into two IQ groups on the basis of scores on the Peabody Picture Vocabulary Test. Each child was tested on the Children's Embedded Figures Test (CEFT), while the mother simultaneously looked at every other CEFT card to aid the child telepathically in finding the solution quicker. High-IQ children completed the tests faster on both ESP and non-ESP targets than low-IQ children. Results were nonsignificant for ESP. Additional analyses were conducted, but overall results were nonsignificant.

126. Ehrenwald, J. (1960). **Schizophrenia, neurotic compliance, and the psi hypothesis.** Psychoanalytic Review, 47, 43-54.

This discusses aspects of psi and its possible relationship to schizophrenia and neurotic processes. It traces psi and psychological aspects back to mother-child symbiotic (telepathic) relationship.

127. Ehrenwald, J. (1971). **Mother-child symbiosis: Cradle of ESP.** Psychoanalytic Review, 58, 455-466.

The article ties the physiological/symbiotic relationship to ESP. "It (symbiosis) suggests that telepathy is in effect the embryological matrix of communication which is later destined to be superseded by speech . . . Telepathy may indeed be a vitally important means of communication, serving the integration and smooth functioning of the mother-child unit, and thereby, its very survival as a viable entity." The author cites several examples of parent-child telepathy and gives explanations.

128. Ehrenwald, J. (1972). **A neurophysiological model of psi phenomena.** Journal of Nervous and Mental Disease, 154, 406-418.

Telepathy and clairvoyance are viewed as extensions of a normal perceptual process, precognition as the reverse of retrospective memory, and PK as an extension of motoric abilities. The author traces psi phenomena to a symbiotic mother-child relationship which becomes repressed and substituted for by "normal" perceptual and motoric processes through development. Psi may then re-emerge under such conditions as trance, hypnosis, dreaming, or severe stress.

129. Ermacora, G. B. (1895). **Telepathic dreams experimentally induced.** Proceedings of the Society for Psychical Research, 11, 235-308.

A cousin of the author (age four) took part over a three-month period in telepathically induced dreams via the author's spirit control. The article recounts the child's ability to see the control spirit as well. The author was the percipient through automatic writing, while the child acted as "sensorial agent" while awake, but unconscious of what was happening.

130. FitzHerbert, J. (1960). **Role of extra-sensory perception in early childhood.** Journal of Mental Science, 106, 1560-1567.

Telepathic occurrences between mother and child, going back as far as prenatal and even pre-embryonal memories, are discussed. Inherited memories, innate knowledge, and response to the unconscious feelings of others (particularly of children to their mothers) are considered along psychoanalytic and paranormal lines.

131. FitzHerbert, J. (1961). **Extrasensory perception in early childhood.** International Journal of Parapsychology, 3, 81-95.

The article gives a perspective of ESP in terms of the mother-child relationship, with psychological and physiological considerations.

132. Gavilon Fontanet, F. (1976). **Los gemelos y su enigma de comunicacion psiquica. [Twins and their enigma of psychic communication.]** Psi Comunicacion, 2, 47-52.

The Spanish Parapsychology Society conducted some experiments with four-year-old girl twins who had demonstrated spontaneous phenomena. In the subjects' home, each twin, in a different room, was presented with stimuli such as odor, light, or cards to see if the other twin gave similar responses or guessed targets correctly. Qualitative analyses considered most of the tests successful.

133. Hansel, C. E. M. (1960). **Experiments on telepathy in children: A reply to Sir Cyril Burt.** British Journal of Statistical Psychology, 13, 175-178.

This is further debate on the validity of results obtained by Soal and Bowden in their work with two 13-year-old boys considered telepathic. (See additional listings, this section: Burt, 1959, 1960; Nicol, 1960; Thouless, 1961; and Book Reviews.)

134. Louwerens, N. G. (1960). **ESP experiments with nursery school children in the Netherlands.** Journal of Parapsychology, 24, 75-93.

A total of 684 pupils (ages 4-6 1/2) in Dutch nursery schools took part in an ESP experiment. Targets were five colored pictures of toys (doll, ball, motor truck, set of blocks, deer) at which the teacher looked. The study yielded highly significant overall results. Girls had significantly higher overall scores than boys, although certain classes had outstanding exceptions to this. Ten classes (420 children) were tested by the author, instead of the teacher, resulting in chance scores. This finding suggests the possibility that differences in the personality of the senders and their relationship to the pupils might be important factors in scoring.

135. MacKenzie, A. (1969). **Ostensible mother-child ESP.** Journal of the Society for Psychical Research, 45, 165-167.

This describes events as told to the author of a mother's anxious feelings concerning her daughter, separated from her by a great distance. No reasons for anxiety were known prior to the mother's concerns. After the experience, the mother learned of events in her daughter's life relating to the anxiety, suggesting it to be indicative of mother-child ESP.

136. Murphy, G. & Anderson, M. (1959). **Experimental objectives of the Anderson-White work with school children.** Journal of Parapsychology, 23, 133-135.

Correspondence by Murphy and Anderson relates to various methodological issues in part of the Anderson-White research.

137. Newman, H. H. (1949). **Telepathy between twins.** Journal of the American Society for Psychical Research, 43, 108-111.

This mentions incidences of telepathy between fraternal

and identical twins. One case of school-age boys is mentioned.

138. Nicol, B. H. (1960). **The Jones boys: A case for telepathy not proven.** Journal of the American Society for Psychical Research, 54, 118-135.

This raises issues and strong negative conclusions concerning the validity of Soal and Bowden's two-year investigation of two boys alleged to be telepathic. The author feels that telepathy was not proved conclusively, as the possibility for sensory cues was never eliminated. (See additional listings, this section: Burt, 1959, 1960; Hansel, 1960; Thouless, 1961; and Book Reviews.)

139. Reeves, M. P. & Rhine, J. B. (1942). **Exceptional scores in ESP tests and the Conditions. I. The case of Lillian.** Journal of Parapsychology, 6, 164-173.

Twenty-one children (12 girls, 9 boys; ages 6-13) were given five ESP test procedures. Statistically significant scores of one child on GESP are discussed.

140. Rhine, L. E. (1956). **The relationship of agent and percipient in spontaneous telepathy.** Journal of Parapsychology, 20, 1-32. (Children mentioned intermittently on pp. 10, 12-17, 29-30.)

This recounts several spontaneous child telepathy cases and one child clairvoyance case.

141. Ruggieri, B. A. (1967). **Pediatric telepathy.** Corrective Psychiatry, 13, 187-195.

The author recounts his own telepathic experiences as a psychiatrist with his young patients (ages infancy to 17).

142. Schwarz, B. E. (1961). **Telepathic events in a child between 1 and 3 1/2 years of age.** International Journal of Parapsychology, 3, 5-47.

This describes 91 cases of telepathy involving the author's wife, daughter, son, and self. It lists many reported events of presumed telepathy. Some are suggestive, some very doubtful. Compilation of all possible telepathic episodes revealed 41 occurrences between father and daughter. There was no considerable difference between parents in type of material transmitted, and the peak of frequency of telepathic episodes occurred at times when the father was finishing some psychical investigation.

143. Shields, E. (1962). **Comparison of children's guessing ability (ESP) with personality characteristics.** Journal of Parapsychology, 26, 200-210.

Children (ages 6-14) referred because of behavioral, learning, or emotional difficulties, took part in two experiments. In the first, twenty-one children were given a battery of personality and intellectual tests for classification as either "withdrawn" or "not withdrawn." An ESP game using Popeye picture cards was administered, with half the runs for clairvoyance and the other half for GESP. The withdrawn group scored marginally significantly below chance. The not-withdrawn group scored significantly above chance. The difference in rate of scoring between the two groups was also significant. In the second experiment, 98 children were divided into withdrawn and not-withdrawn groups and given a matching ESP test. The withdrawn group was slightly, but not significantly, above chance, and the not-withdrawn group was above chance to a significant degree. The total combined not-withdrawn group yielded a significant difference compared to the withdrawn group. Additional analyses were conducted.

144. Shields, E. (1976). **Severely mentally retarded children's psi ability** [Summary]. In J. D. Morris, W. G. Roll, & R. L. Morris (Eds.), Research in Parapsychology 1975 (pp. 135-139). Metuchen, NJ: Scarecrow Press.

Twenty-five children (ages 7-21) diagnosed as trainable mentally retarded (IQs 30-63), having Down's syndrome (IQs 21-71), and having no medical diagnosis (IQs 32-73) were tested for telepathy and clairvoyance. All three groups scored significantly on telepathy tests. Clairvoyance scores approached significance. Neither telepathy nor clairvoyance scores correlated with age or IQ, and the three diagnostic groups did not differ markedly from each other.

145. Shrager, E. F. (1978). **The effect of sender-receiver relationship and associated personality variables on ESP scoring in young children.** Journal of the American Society for Psychical Research, 72, 35-47.

Thirty-eight children, ages 3 1/2--5 1/2, were tested in two telepathy sessions, once with their own mother and once with a stranger as agent. ESP scores with the stranger-sender were significantly lower than ESP scores with their own mother ($p < .03$). Scores with the stranger showed psi-missing ($p < .04$). Scores with their own mother as agent were slightly but nonsignificantly higher than chance. With the stranger agent, extraversion was significantly correlated with ESP scores ($p < .04$). Additional analyses were conducted.

146. Spinelli, E. (1977). **The effects of chronological age on GESP ability** [Summary]. In J. D. Morris, W. G. Roll, & R. L. Morris (Eds.), *Research in Parapsychology 1976* (pp. 122-124). Metuchen, NJ: Scarecrow Press.

A total of 1,000 subjects in 10 age groups, (ages ranging from 3 to 70) were tested. Each group consisted of 50 males and 50 females, tested in teams of two. The three groups below age eight obtained scores significantly above chance ($p < .001$). The youngest subjects (ages 3-4) scored significantly higher than the other two groups ($p < .001$), and the middle group (ages 4-5) significantly higher than the oldest of the three groups (5-8 years) ($p < .001$). There was no significant difference between male and female scores. In a replication, children scored significantly higher ($p < .001$) than college students.

147. Spinelli, E. (1983). **Paranormal cognition: Its summary and implications.** *Parapsychology Review*, *14*, 5-8. (See also Spinelli, 1987; Blackmore, 1984.)

The author proposes a theory of paranormal cognition that places emphasis on cognitive aspects. Research findings are presented showing that paranormal cognition is strongly related to and affected by both chronological age and intelligence. Paranormal cognition, therefore, is more actively and successfully used at earlier age levels.

148. Spinelli, E. (1984). **"ESP in young children": Spinelli replies.** *Journal of the Society for Psychical Research*, *52*, 371-377. (See also Spinelli, 1987; Blackmore, 1984.)

The author replies to S. Blackmore's comments on his child telepathy research conducted from 1974-1978. This article reviews procedures used and defends the results against each of the criticisms made. Precautions used against target selection bias are delineated.

149. Spinelli, E. (1987). **Child development and GESP: A summary.** Parapsychology Review, 18, 8-11. (See critique by S. Blackmore, 1984.)

The author suggests that children who are in the early stages of conscious self-development will manifest greater GESP. Once a stable, conscious self-identity has been formed, GESP will be greatly reduced. His experiments with subjects 3-70 years old are included.

150. Taves, E. (1944). **Some paranormal experiences of hyperthyroid subjects.** Journal of the American Society for Psychical Research, 38, 132-138.

The article reports a spontaneous telepathy case involving a 3 1/2-year-old boy.

151. Teng, L. C. (1981). **Letter.** Journal of the Society for Psychical Research, 51, 181-183.

A report on a 12-year-old boy with "exceptional faculties" -- when paper balls with writing on them are put in his ears, he can write down the balls' written contents on separate paper. The boy describes seeing images of the writing, which appear more quickly when he is in a good mood and warmed up.

152. Thouless, R. H. (1961). **Were the Jones boys signalling by Morse code?** Journal of the American Society for Psychical Research, 55, 24-28.

The article introduces possibility of ultrasonic signaling occurring between the two "psychic boys" discussed by Soal and Bowden. The author concludes that his signaling hypothesis is not supported. (See also Burt, 1959, 1960; Hansel, 1960; Nicol, 1960; and Book Reviews.)

153. Tolaas, J. (1986). **Vigilance theory and psi. Part I. Ethological and phylogenetic aspects.** Journal of the American Society for Psychical Research, 80, 357-373.

The REM state of sleep associated with dreaming in humans is discussed from the phylogenetic and ontogenetic perspective. It is proposed that telepathy is a form of communication that may have originated in the intrauterine period of mother-fetus symbiosis and continues in the early postnatal period.

154. Tornatore, R. P. (1984). **The use of fantasy in a children's ESP experiment** [Summary]. In R. A. White & R. S. Broughton (Eds.), Research in Parapsychology 1983 (pp. 102-103). Metuchen, NJ: Scarecrow Press.

Two groups, each consisting of six pairs of children (second graders), were matched for sex, age, and I.Q. Half of each pair was the agent in a telepathy experiment, using picture slides as targets. After five trials, the children reversed roles. The second group was given similar procedures, with the addition of a fantasy scenario using the "E.T." story to aid in telepathic communication. Results were non-significant for both groups, but in the predicted direction. The small sample may have contributed to the nonsignificant results.

155. Tyrrell, G. N. M. (1948). **Family telepathy.** Journal of the Society for Psychical Research, 34, 196-204.

This recounts five different case incidences involving children (ages 1, 3 1/2, 4 1/2, 5, 10, and 12) with their mother or family members (pp. 201-203).

156. Van Busschbach, J. G. (1955). **A further investigation on an investigation on ESP in school children.** Journal of Parapsychology, 19, 73-81.

Secondary school pupils (ages 12-20) took part in an ESP test. The results of this series were at chance level. A second series was then run with both primary and secondary school children, with a teacher, a stranger, and a pupil alternately serving as agent. Overall results were significant because of the high positive scoring of primary school students. The best scoring was with the teacher as sender. Secondary school pupils scored close to chance level with all senders. All three series combined (a total of 132,780 trials) gave a statistically significant deviation. Primary school students scored significantly higher than secondary school students, and the teacher as agent resulted in significantly higher scoring than the other agents. A total of 31 secondary classes with 669 pupils were in the first experiment, with 907 primary students and 268 secondary students in the second experiment.

157. Van Busschbach, J. G. (1956). **An investigation of ESP between teacher and pupils in American schools.** Journal of Parapsychology, 26, 71-80.

An investigation in American 5th and 6th grades of ESP between teachers and pupils, repeats investigations in Dutch schools. The teacher, concealed and located in the rear of the classroom, looked at the card selected at random from a set of five, while the pupil attempted to identify the card. Ten trials were made with each of three different sets of cards (one set having five arithmetic symbols, another having five colors, and the third having five names of common objects). Thirty trials were given for each session. The total number of students was 1,207, with 40 teachers. Results were statistically significant.

158. Van Busschbach, J. G. (1959). **An investigation of ESP in first and second grades of Dutch schools.** Journal of Parapsychology, 23, 227-237.

In the present test, a total of 51,624 trials were conducted with 1,434 first and second graders (ages 6-8) in two different cities. Children were asked to guess targets at which the teacher was looking, as she sat concealed from their view. A choice of one out of three possible targets was given, with three types of targets used (geometric shapes, ordinary objects, colors). There were statistically significant results in different aspects of the experiment. First graders scored significantly higher than second graders, and girls scored higher than boys. Additional analyses are discussed.

159. Van Busschbach, J. G. (1961). **An investigation of ESP in first and second grades in American schools.** Journal of Parapsychology, 25, 161-174.

This research was a continuation of former work by the same author. Subjects were first- and second-grade pupils in public and private elementary schools. The pupils tried to guess pictures, symbols, and colors looked at by the teacher, who was concealed from view. The first half of the experiment gave positive scores, while the second half yielded negative scores. Overall results were nonsignificant. There was a significant difference between the two halves of the study. There was a total of 1,408 pupils and 52 different teachers.

160. Van de Castle, R. L. (1959). **A review of ESP tests carried out in the classroom.** International Journal of Parapsychology, 1, 84-99.

This thoroughly reviews studies of Van Busschbach, Anderson, and White, and several others who tried either to repeat or to modify various studies by the first two authors. It presents a general overview of the experiments and discusses the implications that the work has for the field of parapsychology.

161. Vasse, P. & Vasse, C. (1955). **PK and ESP experiments with Martie Vasse.** Proceedings of the First International Conference of Parapsychological Studies (pp. 27-29). NY: Parapsychology Foundation.

This describes the Vasses' continuing ESP and PK experiments with their daughter, (age 3 1/2). They found that when ESP was high, PK was high too. Tests were administered for both ESP and PK on the same day. A total of 39 ESP runs and 78 PK runs were conducted, with 264 ESP hits (chance 195) and 381 PK hits (chance 312).

162. West, D. J. (1963). **A veridical dream of a mother of her sick child.** Journal of the Society for Psychical Research, 42, 62-64.

This contains excerpts from letters about a dream a mother had of her 2 1/2-year-old daughter. The mother had gone abroad, and five weeks later she had a nightmare that her child was in terrible pain, crying and being put into an ambulance. The mother wrote a letter warning the grandmother to be careful with the child. A telegram was received a few days later that the child had been rushed to the hospital the night of the mother's nightmare.

Books and Articles

163. Rhine, L. E. (1968). Hidden Channels of the Mind. NY: William Sloane, pp. 148-160.

Chapter 7 relates information on ESP in childhood. "The interesting general fact that emerges from studying children is that their experiences, though simpler, still are similar both in form and type to those of adults. It seems that ESP may be 'there' even in childhood." (p. 160).

Reviewed by: 1) Das Gupta, N. K. (1961-62). Indian Journal of Parapsychology, 3, 52-54. 2) Fisk, G. W. (1961). Journal of Parapsychology, 25, 271-276.

164. Schwarz, B. E. (1971). Parent-Child Telepathy. NY: Garrett Publications.

Countless incidents of telepathy between the author and his young children are recounted and discussed, primarily anecdotal material.

165. Schwarz, B. E. (1972). **Family telepathy.** Psychic, 3(5), 16-19.

The article cites several examples of continuing family telepathic experiences from 1,520 documented incidents over a fifteen-year period. Events mainly involve the author and his wife, their son, and their daughter, from the children's infancy through ages 15 (daughter) and 13 (son).

166. Soal, S. G. & Bowden, H. T. (1959). The Mind Readers. London: Faber and Faber; NY: Doubleday, 1960 (revised ed.).

This controversial book deals with boys, age 13, who are cousins. On telepathy tests, one boy scored seven hits out of 25 consistently, but when monetary rewards were offered (up to $40 each), his scores suddenly became 10s, 11s, and two runs of 15 hits. Over the next two days, the boys averaged over 12 hits per run. (See also Burt, 1959, 1960; Hansel, 1960; Nicol, 1960; Thouless, 1961; and Book Reviews.)

Reviewed by: 1) Birge, T. (1960). **Telepathy experiment in Wales.** International Journal of Parapsychology, 2, 5-23. 2) Pratt, J. G. (1960). Journal of Parapsychology, 24, 53-63.

167. Tauber, E. S. & Green, M. Prelogical experience. NY: Basic Books, 1959.

This book includes a chapter on subthreshold processes mentioning extrasensory perception. Authors try to tie ESP into developmental levels. The book raises the question of whether the use of prelogical faculties for ESP is a regression to an infantile state.

Reviewed by: Matthews, E. de P. (1961). Journal of the American Society for Psychical Research, 55, 36-39.

B. Junior high schoolers (13-15 years)

168. Baggally, W. W. (1913-14). **Report on experiments with "Amy Joyce."** Journal of the Society for Psychical Research, 6, 168-173.

This is a discussion of telepathy experiments conducted with Amy Joyce. No firm conclusions are drawn, but some scattered evidence of telepathy was noted, and further experiments, to be conducted by others, were recommended. (See Feilding & Johnson, 1913-14; Hill, 1913-14; and Lodge, 1913-14.)

169. Barrett, W. F. (1882-1883). **First report on thought-reading.** Proceedings of the Society for Psychical Research, 1, 13-34.

This reports on the five Creery girls (ages 10-17) and a young servant girl, each of whom was able to correctly guess a card or other object hidden in her absence. Testing was conducted in the Creery house with a child as the subject and parents along with other guests as agent. The study lasted six days with 382 trials, of which 127 were successful on the first attempt and 56 correct on the second guess. (See Creery, 1882; Gurney, 1882, 1888; and Stewart, 1882.)

170. Barrett, W. F. (1882-1883). **Appendix to report on thought-reading.** Proceedings of the Society for Psychical Research, 1, 47-65.

This mentions cases of children and adults evidencing telepathy, as well as telepathic incidents with hypnotized subjects. The material is anecdotal rather than experimental.

171. Creery, A. M. (1882-1883). **Note on thought-reading.** Proceedings of the Society for Psychical Research, 1, 43-46.

The article goes into detail about how the Creery children and servant received their telepathic/clairvoyant impressions. (See Barrett, 1882; Gurney, 1882, 1888; and Stewart, 1882.)

172. Drake, R. M. (1938). **An unusual case of extrasensory perception.** Journal of Parapsychology, 2, 184-198.

An 11-year-old retarded boy was found to repeat words and numbers thought by his mother spontaneously. ESP cards were utilized with similar results. A significant average of 7.6 hits per run was obtained with mechanical signals operated by the experimenter. The accuracy of the responses to both verbal and mechanical signals declined rapidly toward the end of the study.

173. Ehrenwald, J. (1954). **Telepathy and the child-parent relationship.** Journal of the American Society for Psychical Research, 48, 43-55.

The paper cites various incidents of parent-child telepathy and cases reported by other psychiatrists. Each case is analyzed in terms of psychoanalytic and parapsychological aspects.

174. Feilding, E. & Johnson, A. (1913-1914). **Report on some experiments in thought-transference.** Journal of the Society for Psychical Research, 6, 164-168.

This reports experiments carried out with supposedly telepathic Amy Joyce at age 14. Results were not significant enough to conclude whether she was telepathic or not. Experimenters found that she "habitually and very cleverly availed herself of any opportunity of normal vision which might present itself." (See Baggally, 1913; Hill, 1913; and Lodge, 1913.)

175. Gurney, E. (1882-1883). **Second report on thought-transference.** Proceedings of the Society for Psychical Research, 1, 70-98.

This discusses a series of 10 consecutive experiments carried out over 10 days with Mary, 17, Alice, 15, and Mared, 13 (Creery sisters). The percentage of success in these cases was not appreciably above average. Additional tests when the two sisters were in Dublin were carried out. (See Barrett, 1888; Creery, 1882; Gurney, 1888; and Stewart, 1882.)

176. Gurney, E. (1888-1889). **Note relating to some of the published experiments in thought-transference.** Proceedings of the Society for Psychical Research, 5, 269-270.

This reports experiments conducted with two of the Creery sisters (one as agent, other as subject) in which they were found to be using a code of signals. A third child confessed to a certain amount of signaling in the earlier series. The author concludes that "the recent detection must throw discredit on the results of all previous trials in which one or more of the sisters shared in the agency." (See Barrett, 1882; Creery, 1882; Gurney, 1882; and Stewart, 1882.)

177. Hearne, K. M. (1981). **Visually evoked responses and "ESP": Failure to replicate previous findings.** Journal of the Society for Psychical Research, 51, 145-147.

Results with 16 subject-agent pairs (ages 13-40) were nonsignificant in an experiment involving visually evoked response and ESP. The amplitude of a negative peak (from EEG recordings) .65 msec after the unpatterned photic stimulation of the subject appeared to vary, depending on whether or not the agent was simultaneously viewing the subject's photograph that was tachistoscopically shown. For both groups the amplitude-shift was opposite.

178. Hill, J. A. (1913-1914). **Note on the experiments with "Amy Joyce."** Journal of the Society for Psychical Research, 6, 173-175.

Mr. Percy Lund administered experiments to Amy Joyce. He found that Amy could name six or seven cards successively with great rapidity, then would be at a loss, as though she had bursts of power. She was also successful in reproducing drawings (square, circle, six-pointed star, cross) which the experimenter drew from the opposite end of the room. Mr. Lund felt results were conclusive evidence of some supernormal faculty on the part of Amy Joyce. (See Baggally, 1913; Feilding & Johnson, 1913; Lodge, 1913.)

179. Lodge, O. (1913-1914). **Report on a case of telepathy.** Journal of the Society for Psychical Research, 6, 102-111.

The author conducted detailed experiments using cards and letters with 13-year-old Amy Joyce, who showed evidence of telepathy. (See Baggally, 1913; Feilding & Johnson, 1913; and Hill, 1913.)

180. Randall, J. L. (1972). **Group ESP experiments with schoolboys.** Journal of Parapsychology, 36, 133-143. (Reprinted as **Experimentos de ESP con un grupo de escolares.** Cuadernos de Parapsicologia, 1972, 5, 1-11.)

An ESP pilot study with 29 grammar school boys (age 14) completed two runs of GESP test with the teacher as sender and two runs of clairvoyance using ESP cards as targets. Overall results were nonsignificant, but the subject variance was significant ($p < .017$). Also, a positive correlation was found between ESP and clairvoyance scores ($p < .03$). Results of a questionnaire yielded that eight significant ESP scorers suffered from hay fever. Significantly high subject variance was found on the Junior Eysenck Personality Inventory for high-neurotic and high-extrovert scorers. A second experiment with 31 subjects yielded similar results. Overall scoring was nonsignificant, but subject variance was significant, as was the correlation between ESP and clairvoyance. Hay fever sufferers again scored above chance, and high-extrovert and neurotic subjects showed high subject variance.

181. Shields, E. (1962). **Comparison of children's guessing ability with personality characteristics.** Journal of Parapsychology, 26, 200-210.

Children (ages 6-14) referred because of behavioral, learning, or emotional difficulties, took part in two experiments. In the first, 21 children were given a battery of personality and intellectual tests for classification as either "withdrawn" or "not withdrawn." An ESP game using Popeye picture cards was administered, with half the runs for clairvoyance and the other half for GESP. The withdrawn group scored marginally significantly below chance. The not-withdrawn group scored significantly above chance. The difference in the rate of scoring between the two groups was also significant. In the second experiment, 98 children were divided into withdrawn and not-withdrawn groups and given a matching ESP test. The withdrawn group was slightly, but not significantly, above chance, and the not-withdrawn group was above chance to a significant degree. The total combined not-withdrawn group yielded a significant difference compared to the withdrawn group. Additional analyses were conducted.

182. Shields, E. (1976). **Severely mentally retarded children's psi ability** [Summary]. In J. D. Morris, W. G. Roll, & R. L. Morris (Eds.), Research in Parapsychology 1975 (pp. 135-139). Metuchen, NJ: Scarecrow Press.

Twenty-five children (ages 7-21) diagnosed as trainable mentally retarded (IQs 30-63), having Down's syndrome (IQs 21-71), and having no medical diagnosis (IQs 32-73) were tested for telepathy and clairvoyance. All three groups scored significantly on telepathy tasks. Clairvoyance scores approached significance. Neither telepathy nor clairvoyance scores correlated with age or IQ, and the three diagnostic groups did not differ markedly from each other.

183. Stewart, B. (1882-1883). **Note on thought-reading.** Proceedings of the Society for Psychical Research, 1, 35-42.

This article adds corroboration through experiments to confirm Barrett's positive findings of telepathy with the Creery children. The experiments are similar to those used by Barrett. (See Barrett, 1882; Creery, 1882; Gurney, 1882, 1888.)

184. Van Busschbach, J. G. (1953). **An investigation of extrasensory perception in school children.** Journal of Parapsychology, 17, 210-214.

Cards marked with three kinds of targets (arithmetical symbols, colors, and words were used to test 673 Dutch primary school children (ages 10-12) for ESP. The 29,190 trials gave overall statistically significant results ($p < .005$). Only the arithmetical symbols were independently significant.

185. Van Busschbach, B. J. (1955). **A further investigation on an investigation of ESP in school children.** Journal of Parapsychology, 19, 73-81.

Secondary school pupils (ages 12-20) took part in an ESP test. The results of this series were at chance level. A second series was then run with both primary and secondary school children, with a teacher, a stranger, and a pupil alternately serving as agent. Overall results were significant because of the high positive scoring of primary school students. The best scoring was with the teacher as sender. Secondary school pupils scored close to chance level with all senders. All three series combined (a total of 132,780 trials) gave a statistically significant deviation. Primary school students scored significantly higher than secondary school students, and the teacher as agent resulted in significantly higher scoring than the other agents. A total of 31 secondary classes with 669 pupils were in the first experiment, with 907 primary students and 268 secondary students in the second experiment.

186. Weisinger, C. (1973). **Two ESP experiments in the classroom.** Journal of Parapsychology, 37, 76-77.

A total of 325 German and Swiss boys (ages 8-15) had to guess the numbers 0 - 9 as targets for two runs, with their teacher as telepathic agent. Overall results were nonsignificant with no correlation found between ESP and children's attitudes toward the teacher or the teacher-child attitude. The teacher's attitude toward parapsychology significantly correlated with the ESP score of the class ($p = .01$). Two additional experiments with children as agents were significant ($p < .0004$, $p < .009$). A reanalysis of data showed significant results of spontaneous psi communication among children. Children tended to take psi information from the most popular classmates ($p < .005$).

In a second series, 451 boys (ages 7-15) were given a clairvoyance card task. Subjects thought they were guessing a down-through deck of 25 cards, when the deck actually contained blank cards. The real targets were, unknown to the subjects, in close proximity to one of the popular classmates. Results were significant ($p = .0032$).

187. White, R. A. & Angstadt, J. (1963). **Student preferences in a two classroom GESP experiment with two student-agents acting simultaneously.** Journal of the American Society for Psychical Research, 57, 32-42.

An ESP talk was given a few days before the ESP experiment involving a total of 53 junior high schoolers. One representative was elected by secret ballot to act as agent for the class. Agents from each of the two classes participated. Results showed younger subjects more successful than older; girls scored better than boys; boys did better when agent was a girl; and girls did better when agent was a boy. A cash reward was offered to the highest scorer.

188. White, R. A. & Angstadt, J. (1963). **A second classroom GESP experiment with student-agents acting simultaneously.** Journal of the American Society for Psychical Research, 57, 227-232.

An introductory talk was given a few days before an ESP experiment with four classes of ninth graders (ages 13-16). There were 24 students in Group I, 29 in Group II, 12 in Group III, and 28 in Group IV, for a total of 93 students. A total of 4,650 guesses based on 50 calls each was conducted. Results generally were nonsignificant, with students of the opposite sex from the agent scoring in the predicted direction, but not significantly.

C. High schoolers (15-17 years)

189. Anderson, M. L. & White, R. A. (1958). **ESP score level in relation to students' attitude toward teacher-agents acting simultaneously.** Journal of Parapsychology, 22, 20-28.

Two teachers and 51 high schoolers took part in an ESP experiment. The students were unaware that two different target decks were used with each teacher as agent. After the tests, students were asked to name which of all the teachers they liked best and to name three others whom they would prefer as a teacher. Results showed that when the teacher was on the "best liked" or the "preferred" list, students' ESP scores were significantly above chance.

190. Anderson, M. L. & White, R. A. (1958). **The relationship between changes in student attitude and ESP scoring.** Journal of Parapsychology, 22, 167-174.

ESP tests and a questionnaire of the teacher's and the pupils' attitudes were given at the beginning and end of the semester to 29 high schoolers. Results showed that changes in the teacher's attitude toward the pupil, as well as changes in their mutual attitudes, were not associated with significant changes in ESP scores. However, changes in attitude of the students to the teacher were significantly related to changes in level of ESP scoring.

191. Barron, F. & Mordkoff, A. M. (1968). **An attempt to relate creativity to possible extrasensory empathy as measured by physiological arousal in identical twins.** Journal of the American Society for Psychical Research, 62, 73-79.

No significant results were reported when nine pairs of identical twins were tested for physiological evidence (skin resistance, pulse, and respiration) of extrasensory empathy. One set of twins in the sample was high school age.

192. Beloff, J., Cowles, M., & Bate, D. (1969). **A GSR-ESP experiment.** Proceedings of the Parapsychological Association, 6, 13-14.

Twenty high schoolers (ages 15-17) had their Galvanic Skin Response measured in response to emotive ESP and sensory stimuli (slides). ESP was allowed to operate on an unconscious level on the first run, with the subject encouraged in the second run to produce a telepathic effect with the experimenter as agent. Highly significant results were obtained on the total sensory runs, but nonsensory ESP runs were nonsignificant.

193. Beloff, J., Cowles, M., & Bate, D. (1970). **Autonomic reactions to emotive stimuli under sensory and extrasensory conditions of presentation.** Journal of the American Society for Psychical Research, 64, 313-319.

Twenty high schoolers (ages 15-17) were tested for Galvanic Skin Response reactions on being presented unexpectedly with their self-image or own name. Presentation was sensory (via slides) and extrasensory, using photoprints, with one author acting as agent. Scoring was done blind by another author. Sensory runs gave overall significant results with extrasensory runs almost exactly at chance level.

194. Charlesworth, E. A. (1975). **Psi and the imaginary dream** [Summary]. In J. D. Morris, W. G. Roll, & R. L. Morris (Eds.), Research in Parapsychology 1974 (pp. 85-89). Metuchen, NJ: Scarecrow Press.

Sixty college students listened to a 33-minute experimental tape recording which guided them into an altered state of consciousness, during which a combined telepathy experiment was conducted. Results yielded significant psi-hitting. A second experiment using this same tape recording had 14 female and 6 male identical twins and 10 female and 10 male fraternal twins as subject-agents. (Mean age of identical twins 15.3 years; mean age of fraternal twins 16.1 years.) Fraternal twins yielded significant psi-hitting (p = .0125).

195. Eisenberg, H. & Donderi, D. C. (1979). **Telepathic transfer of emotional information in humans.** Journal of Psychology, 103, 19-43.

Thirty-seven students, plus 17 housewives, teachers, and secretaries (ages 14-44) were paired in a telepathy experiment, using emotionally stimulating films as targets. Forced-choice photo-ranking was used for judging. Two control groups totaling 45 subjects were tested on the photo-ranking task under nontelepathic conditions. Further correlations between personality, attitude scales, and success in telepathy suggest fatigue and related factors improved the photo-ranking task performance. Performance on a particular stimulus film was significantly correlated with personality test responses, rather than with the overall performance. A smaller replication study supported these conclusions.

196. Foster, E. B. (1956). **A re-examinaton of Dr. Soal's "clairvoyance" data.** *Journal of Parapsychology*, *20*, 110-120.

The author questions whether Soal, in his GESP investigation of a Spanish girl, might not have overlooked indications of clairvoyance. The author notes that Langdon-Davies obtained results that were as high for clairvoyance as for GESP. However, Soal and Bateman's work yielded only chance results with clairvoyance and significantly positive evidence with GESP. The author questions whether Soal and his associates may have introduced some psychological factor that allows the operation of ESP under GESP conditions but inhibits its function under conditions allowing only clairvoyance to occur. (See listing this section: Langdon-Davies, Bateman, and Soal, 1955. Also see Clairvoyance, High Schoolers.)

197. Kubis, J. G. & Rouke, F. L. (1937). **An experimental investigation of telepathic phenomena in twins.** *Journal of Parapsychology*, *1*, 163-171.

Six sets of twins (one identical and five fraternal; ages 10-21) were tested for telepathy. The twins were placed in separate rooms and signaled to call the ESP cards looked at by the experimenter. Their calls were compared with both the experimenter's cards and corresponding calls of the other twin. Subjects did not know that the latter check was to be made. No significant number of correspondences between subjects' calls resulted. Two subjects did score significantly high on cards looked at by the experimenter.

198. Langdon-Davies, J. L., Bateman, F., & Soal, S. G. (1955). **ESP tests with a Spanish girl.** *Journal of Parapsychology*, *19*, 155-163.

High-scoring ESP ability in Maria, a 16-year-old Spanish kitchen maid, was tested under informal exploratory conditions. In both tests of clairvoyance and GESP, above chance scores were obtained by Langdon-Davies. However, clairvoyance scores dropped to chance under the testing conducted by Soal and Bateman. Maria continued to score above chance on GESP tests with Soal and Bateman. (See Foster, 1956.)

199. Nvomeysky, A. (1984). **On the possible effect of an experimenter's subliminal or telepathic influence on dermo-optic sensitivity.** PSI Research, 3, 8-15.

A series of color telepathy (CT) experiments done in the USSR since 1960 are reported. A physiological explanation is proposed, suggesting information transfer is related to brain radiations transmitted to one another, similar to those involved in dermo-optic perception (i.e., electrostatic fields, infrared emissions of brain cells, millimeter electromagnetic waves, etc.). The studies showed adolescents (ages 14-15) have a better capacity for CT, and CT decreases with age.

200. Randall, J. L. (1974). **Card-guessing experiment with school boys.** Journal of the Society for Psychical Research, 47, 421-432. (Reprinted in abstract form in Journal of Parapsychology, 1975, 39, 90-91.)

Results of six classroom experiments with 169 high school boys yielded 16 students obtaining ESP scores that were marginally significant ($p < .05$) and six obtaining scores that were highly significant ($p < .01$). There was a general tendency for scores obtained under clairvoyance to be marginally positively correlated ($p = .04$) with scores under GESP conditions. Additionally, students classified as both high-extrovert and high-neurotic on the Junior Eysenck Personality Scale showed high subject variance ($p = .0008$). Subjects classified as both low-extrovert and low-neurotic also obtained significant subject variance ($p = .02$).

201. Randall, J. L. (1974). **An extended series of ESP and PK tests with three English schoolboys.** Journal of the Society for Psychical Research, 47, 485-494.

This reports on extended ESP and PK tests done with three high schoolers who had previously done well in classroom ESP tests. Two subjects repeated their original performance in the predicted direction with significant scores. Each subject also did PK tests moving a gerbil to the left or right side of a box. One subject scored significantly ($p < .036$). Subjects also performed PK with a binary random number generator, but results were nonsignificant. One subject's data showed a chronological decline that was statistically significant ($p < .025$).

202. Recordan, E. G., Stratton, F. J. M., & Peters, R. A. (1968). **Some trials in a case of alleged telepathy.** Journal of the Society for Psychical Research, 44, 390-399.

A 15-year-old mentally retarded boy diagnosed as having Spastic Displegia with congenital cataracts could "see" items beyond his range. ESP tests using one-figure numbers and letters of the alphabet as targets were given with the mother as agent six miles away. Results were significant.

203. Rivers, O. B. (1950). **An exploratory study of the mental health and intelligence of ESP subjects.** Journal of Parapsychology, 14, 267-277.

Two groups of 36 college men and 36 high school boys were given a series of clairvoyance and GESP tests, as well as a mental health analysis. While total ESP scores were statistically significant, the mental health analysis did not prove reliable in selecting good ESP subjects.

204. Sanderson, G. D. (1965). **Report on an experiment on the relationship between teacher-pupil extrasensory transfer and letter grades.** Science Education, 49, 446-452.

A total of 107 high schoolers completed 535 runs of a telepathy experiment using Zener cards. The teacher acted as agent. Overall results for each class and as a whole were nonsignificant. Additional analyses are discussed.

205. Sommer, R., Osmond, H., & Pancyr, L. (1961). **Selection of twins for ESP experimentation.** International Journal of Parapsychology, 3, 55-73.

A survey was conducted of 14 pairs of twins and 7 single twins (where only one of the pair was available) from Western Canada. Ages ranged from 16-50 years, with the majority of twins in their late teens. Twelve twins (8 identical, 4 fraternal) felt that they could communicate by thought with the other, and seven reported being able to sense when a twin was in difficulty even though geographically separated.

206. White, R. A. & Angstadt, J. (1961). **Student preferences shown in a two-classroom GESP experiment with two-student agents acting simultaneously.** Journal of Parapsychology, 25, 281-282.

Fifty-five students in two high school biology classes were tested for telepathy. A student from each class whom the majority in each class felt close to and liked best was selected by secret ballot. These two representatives simultaneously looked at different sets of 20 playing cards, while other students in each class tried to guess the cards at which their own representative was looking. A prize was offered to the class scoring the highest on their own representative's targets. Both classes scored significantly high on their own representatives' targets (p = .0008). The Period 1 class scored higher than the Period 5 class. In both classes, there was a tendency for girls to score higher if the preferred agent was a boy and for boys to score higher if the preferred agent was a girl (p = .002).

207. White, R. A. & Angstadt, J. (1965). **A review of results and new experiments bearing on teacher-selection methods in the Anderson-White high school experiments.** Journal of the American Society for Psychical Research, 59, 56-84.

This reviews the experiments conducted with 476 students and 15 teachers to study the relationship of teacher-pupil attitudes to ESP scoring results.

III. PRECOGNITION

III. PRECOGNITION

A. Pre-school/elementary age (infancy to 12 years)

208. Anderson, M. L. (1960). **A year's testing program with a class of public school pupils.** Journal of Parapsychology, 24, 314.

Two clairvoyance tests and one precognition test (launching of a missile) were administered by a teacher to her fourth- and fifth-grade pupils. The two clairvoyance series together yielded significant results. The precognitive test was slightly below chance.

209. Anderson, M. L. (1966). **The use of fantasy in testing for extrasensory perception.** Journal of the American Society for Psychical Research, 60, 150-163.

This article reviews three separate studies conducted with elementary school children. The first involved clairvoyance and precognition tests in which 32 students "tuned in" on the "music of outer space." The second had 28 students who mentally "launched" a mythical missile. The third, involving the entire elementary school, was a clairvoyance test around mentally launching, orbiting, and recovering a space capsule. This last test explored the relationship of ESP scoring and creativity, as assessed by teacher rating. Each study had significant results.

210. Anderson, M. L. & Gregory, E. (1959). **A two-year program of tests for clairvoyance and precognition with a class of public school pupils.** Journal of Parapsychology, 23, 149-177.

Fifth-grade students (32), having scored well on previous ESP tests, were chosen for a two-year experiment. Clairvoyance tests were given the first year, yielding nonsignificant positive results. The second-year tests were cognitive in nature and used the same class, now in the sixth grade, and teacher. Total scores gave positively significant results. Variations in scoring from session to session also yielded highly significant results.

211. Anderson, M. L. & McConell, R. A. (1961). **Fantasy testing for ESP in a fourth and fifth grade class.** Journal of Psychology, 52, 491-503. (Also abstracted in the Journal of Parapsychology, 1962, 26, 135.)

Twenty-eight pupils of a combined fourth- and fifth-grade class were tested for clairvoyance and precognition through purposeful fantasy in the launching of a rocket. A total of 6,620 guesses made in eight sessions yielded overall significant results ($p = .03$).

212. Berger, R. E. (1989). **Discussion: A critical examination of the Blackmore psi experiments.** Journal of the American Society for Psychical Research, 83, 123-144.

Blackmore's psi experiment data base (two experiments with young children) is examined and found to have discrepancies between unpublished reports and published counterparts. Blackmore's claims that her data base shows no evidence of psi are called unfounded. Berger states that no conclusions at all can be drawn from her data base.

Blackmore, S. J. **A critical response to Rick Berger,** 145-154. Blackmore finds Berger's accusations unfounded; where she failed to replicate Spinelli's results with children, she traces the problem to Spinelli's reportage and statistics.

Berger, R. E. **Reply to Blackmore's: "A critical response to Rick Berger."** 155-157. Berger refutes points made by Blackmore.

213. Blackmore, S. (1980). **A study of memory and ESP in young children.** Journal of the Society for Psychical Research, 50, 501-520.

The literature on ESP in children is reviewed and found to show little systematic evidence of a relationship between ESP and age. In a pilot study, 19 playgroup children (ages 3-6) were tested for clairvoyance and GESP, with different colored candies as targets. Results were not significant. In the main experiment, subjects were 48 children from three playgroups (ages 3-5). Children were given memory and preference tests. Targets were colored pictures on white cards. Children took turns as sender and receiver. Results showed no significant correlation of either memory or age of the child with ESP.

214. Drucker, S. A. & Rubin, L. (1975). **In which hand are the M & M's? A preliminary study of ESP in relation to cognitive development and testing environment** [Summary]. In J. D. Morris, W. G. Roll, & R. L. Morris (Eds.), Research in Parapsychology 1974 (pp. 38-40). Metuchen, NJ: Scarecrow Press.

Forty-two children (ages 4-7) were tested for precognition (with M & M candies) and Piaget's Conservation of Liquids test. Twenty-seven were tested at home and fifteen at school. Results showed overall nonsignificant ESP. However, children tested in a home setting had overall significant ($p < .05$) ESP scores, as did children classified as "mixed" according to the Piaget test ($p < .05$).

215. Drucker, S. A. & Drewes, A. A. (1976). **Return of the M & M's: A further study of ESP in relation to cognitive development** [Summary]. In J. D. Morris, W. G. Roll, & R. L. Morris (Eds.), Research in Parapsychology 1975 (pp. 160-162). Metuchen, NJ: Scarecrow Press.

Fifty children (ages 4-7) were tested on two trials for precognition through the use of M & M candies. In addition, a vocabulary IQ test and Piaget's Conservation of Liquids test were given. Results showed high-IQ children obtained statistically significant higher ESP scores on the second of two runs ($p = .01$). Low-IQ children showed statistically significant scores on the first run when compared to their second run ($p < .02$).

216. Drucker, S. A., Drewes, A. A., & Rubin, L. (1977). **ESP in relation to cognitive development and IQ in young children.** Journal of the American Society for Psychical Research, 71, 289-298.

This article summarizes two earlier experiments with a total of 92 children (ages 4-7). Piaget's Conservation of Liquids test and a vocabulary IQ test were administered in conjunction with a two-run precognitive task using M & M candies. Results showed significant ESP results when children were tested at home rather than in school, for high-IQ children vs. low-IQ children, and for "mixed" classifications vs. prelogical or logical groups.

217. Freeman, J. A. (1963). **Boy-girl differences in a group precognition test.** Journal of Parapsychology, 27, 175-181.

A teacher of mentally retarded children (4 girls and 13 boys; ages 10-13) carried out two series of precognitive tests under the author's direction. The test was gamelike, and the ESP task embedded in mimeographed picture booklets. In the first series, there was a significant difference between negative scoring by girls and positive scoring by boys. The second series showed the same trend but was nonsignificant. The overall evaluation for the entire experiment approached significance.

218. Freeman, J. A. (1965). **Differential response of the sexes to contrasting arrangements of ESP target material.** Journal of Parapsychology, 29, 251-258.

A pilot precognitive experiment with 50 girls and 49 boys showed girls scored positively on test material where five picture targets were alike and negatively when all pictures were different. Boys scored in the opposite direction. Three experimental series replicated these findings. The first experiment had 7 girls and 9 boys in elementary school, the second had 13 boys and 11 girls in nursery school, and the third had 16 girls and 9 boys in fifth grade. The total difference between boys and girls was significant ($p < .01$).

219. Freeman, J. A. (1970). **Sex differences in scoring on ESP booklet tests -- a confirmation.** Journal of Parapsychology, 34, 65-66.

Sixth-grade students were tested for ESP on trials where all the targets were alike (using both symbols and words). Results showed girls had more hits on alike targets than trials of five different targets. Boys scored the reverse. In 32 runs (25 trials each) of same target, girls had three hits less than expected by chance. Boys had 14 hits less than chance in 38 runs.

220. Freeman, J. A. (1970). **Ten page booklet tests with elementary school children.** Journal of Parapsychology, 34, 192-196.

A ten-page booklet for precognition was given to 35 sixth-grade children (16 girls and 19 boys). Several pages had trials based on five different words, on one word repeated five times, on five different symbols, or on one symbol repeated five times. Girls scored higher on trials where all the targets were alike (symbols, words), than when there were five different targets. Boys scored the reverse.

221. Johnson, M. (1970). **Teacher-pupil relationship and ESP scoring.** Journal of Parapsychology, 34, 277.

A sixth-grade class performed two 25-trial runs with ESP cards. The first run was a clairvoyance task, while the second run used blank cards and was a precognitive task. The teacher-agent rated students on intelligence, extraversion-introversion, degree of rapport with teacher, and anxiety-proneness. The clairvoyance run yielded positive but nonsignificant results. The precognitive run yielded positive, significant results ($p = .01$), with the combined results being statistically significant ($p < .01$). The correlation between teacher's ratings and students' performance was in the expected direction but nonsignificant.

222. Schmidt, H. & Pantas, L. (1972). **Psi tests with internally different machines.** Journal of Parapsychology, 36, 222-232.

A large group of subjects from elementary school age to adult were individually tested in a group setting. A specially constructed machine would preselect one of four target lights according to an internal electronic generator for each forthcoming precognition trial. By the subject's flipping a switch, a hit was achieved through the subject's previous mental activation of the internally selected target (PK). Results were statistically significant within each of the two trials. A second experiment testing a single high scorer showed similar results.

223. Stevenson, I. (1961). **An example illustrating the criteria and characteristics of precognitive dreams.** Journal of the American Society for Psychical Research, 55, 98-103.

A spontaneous precognitive dream between a mother and her 20-month-old daughter is described and discussed.

224. Weiner, D. H., Haight, J. M., Marion, M. D., & Munson, R. J. (1980). **The possible value of repeated visitation in group testing.** [Summary]. In W. G. Roll (Ed.), Research in Parapsychology 1979 (pp. 177-179). Metuchen, NJ: Scarecrow Press.

This summarizes a study done in an elementary school mini-group teaching situation, with nine fifth and sixth graders in group one (5 males; 4 females) and ten fourth and fifth graders in group two (6 males; 4 females). There was informal competition between boys and girls in all tasks. Session one was precognition, using a random number generator. Results were nonsignificant. Session two was macro-PK, where boys and girls tried to influence the growth of rye seeds on separate trays. Pooled results were significant at $p < .05$. Session three was precognitive, using a random number generator, with prizes to the highest scorer of the group. Boys scored above chance and girls below in group one ($p < .05$); this was reversed in group two ($p < .01$). The authors conclude that repeated visitation combined with prizes can be a successful procedure.

225. Winkelman, M. (1981). **The effect of formal education on extrasensory abilities: The Ozolco Study.** Journal of Parapsychology, 45, 321-336.

Three experiments assess whether or not increase in formal education inhibits ESP abilities. Subjects were 29 children from a rural Mexican village (ages 8-14) with zero to seven years of education. Clairvoyance testing with candy yielded significant results ($p < .005$), while use of marbles in clairvoyance testing was nonsignificant. Precognitive testing with candy was significant at the .05 level, while precognitive testing using marbles was nonsignificant. PK testing using marbles yielded $p < .1$. There were no strong significant differences between males and females. Additional testing of field independence, conservation, math, and years of schooling were correlated. Total ESP correlated negatively with math ($p < .02$), schooling ($p < .03$), conservation, field independence, and age. Similar negative correlations were found with clairvoyance and precognition testing. PK correlated positively with age ($p < .006$).

B. Junior high schoolers (13 to 15 years)

226. Brier, R. M. (1968). **Evidence of precognition in the run scores of the Read Test.** Journal of Parapsychology, 32, 131.

Over 100,000 junior high schoolers responded to a precognition experiment published in Read magazine. Results of an initial 10,000 records indicate boys showed nonsignificant scores, whereas girls scored significantly ($p < .001$). A second additional study with 5,000 girls gave confirmatory results of high scoring ($p < .001$).

227. Brier, R. M. (1969). **A mass school test of precognition.** Journal of Parapsychology, 33, 125-135.

Out of 100,000 junior high schoolers responding to an ESP article and precognition test, a group of 10,059 records showed girls significantly differed from chance ($p < .001$), while boys scored at chance. An additional 7,632 records confirmed the results. Fluctuations in scoring in the four five-trial segments of the run were found. Out of a block of 31 classes, 22 showed boys with significantly more variance ($p < .03$) than girls. The finding was again confirmed in an additional block of 493 classes.

228. Feather, S. R. (1969). **Position effects in a mass precognition test.** Journal of Parapsychology, 33, 72.

Position effects are examined in a sample of 1,940 record sheets from a precognition test given in Read magazine. The successes of both girls and boys showed a U-curve distribution according to four-segments of the 20-trial test. This position effect was also present when data was divided into above-chance and at-or-below chance subjects.

229. Freeman, J. A. (1966). **Sex differences and target arrangements: High-school booklet tests of precognition.** Journal of Parapsychology, 30, 227-235.

A precognition task using a 10-page booklet had targets (symbols and words) arranged in rows containing alike and different targets. The pilot study with 15 girls and 18 boys (junior high school ages) showed girls scoring higher when the rows contained different symbols and same words. Boys scored the reverse. Results of four confirmatory studies (with a total of 96 junior high and high schoolers) were in the expected direction. The difference between the total predicted positive and negative results was statistically significant (p = .0008).

230. Freeman, J. A. (1967). **Sex differences, target arrangements and primary mental abilities.** Journal of Parapsychology, 31, 271-279.

Freeman's 10-page precognitive booklet was administered to 68 junior high schoolers (41 girls and 27 boys) along with two subtests of the Primal Mental Abilities Test (Verbal Meaning and Spatial Relations). Students scoring high on Spatial Relations were found to score high on rows where the targets were the same symbols and different words, and lower on the converse. The difference between these two scores was significant. Students with low Spatial scores had ESP scores in the expected direction but which were nonsignificant. The overall difference between expected positive and negative scores was significant (p = .002).

231. Freeman, J. A. (1968). **Evidence of precognition in sex differences in the Read Test.** Journal of Parapsychology, 32, 133.

A pilot analysis of 31 junior high school classes participating in an ESP experiment from Read magazine suggested that scoring was related to the sex of the student. Boys produced consistently higher segment variance than girls (p < .01). A confirmation analysis supported this trend, with 274 of 493 classes showing the boys to have a higher segment variance than the girls (p < .008).

232. Freeman, J. A. (1968). **Sex differences and primary mental abilities in a group precognition test.** Journal of Parapsychology, 32, 176-182.

This is a replication of a previous test. Thirty-two seventh graders (9 girls and 23 boys) were divided into two groups, high and low scorers on the Spatial Relations subtest of the Primary Mental Abilities Test. Precognitive tests using a ten-page booklet (with two different arrangements of words and symbols) were administered. The high-spatial students scored significantly better, with both groups scoring in the expected direction on word trials ($p = .003$). Both groups scored contrary to expectations on symbol trials.

233. Freeman, J. A. (1968). **Sex differences, target arrangement and primary mental abilities.** Journal of Parapsychology, 32, 291-292.

This is a condensation of the full paper listed above. High-spatial and low-spatial scoring subjects scored in the expected direction on a word trial precognition test ($p = .003$) and contrary on the symbol trials.

234. Freeman, J. A. (1969). **Decline of variance in school precognition tests.** Journal of Parapsychology, 33, 72.

A 12-page precognition booklet was used with junior high schoolers. The booklet was divided into four pages of figures and pictures of circular designs, four pages of angular designs, and the remaining four pages of designs containing both circular and angular designs. No sex differences were noted in scoring. Similar significant decline across three segments of the test, with the first segment showing the largest variance, was noted.

235. Freeman, J. A. (1970). **Race differences in scoring on ESP booklet tests. A first finding.** Journal of Parapsychology, 34, 65.

A class of eighth-grade black students were given precognitive booklet tests plus verbal and spatial subtests of the Thurstone Primary Mental Abilities test. High-spatial girls and boys scored as expected, as did high-verbal boys and girls. The difference between the two groups of high scorers was statistically significant ($p = .015$). However, unlike previous research, students did not differentiate between trials of different or same target arrangement. Results are similar to elementary school students tested rather than those of junior high schoolers.

236. Freeman, J. A. (1970). **Sex differences in ESP response as shown by the Freeman Picture-Figure test.** *Journal of Parapsychology*, *34*, 37-46.

This study examines previous research using scores on verbal and spatial subtests of Primary Mental Abilities (PMA) test. Two classes of junior high schoolers (25 and 28 subjects) were given ESP targets in booklet form containing pages of five geometric figures or five pictures of objects along with the Reason subtest of the PMA. On some pages, rows had five targets all the same, while on other pages, there were five different targets in each row. Three analyses were conducted with significant results discussed.

237. Freeman, J. A. (1970). **Shift in scoring direction with junior high school students: A summary.** *Journal of Parapsychology*, *34*, 275.

Five seventh-grade classes were given a precognitive test along with the Spatial Relations test of the Primary Mental Abilities test. The ESP scores of eight of the ten groups (the five classes were divided by sex) were in the opposite direction of the prediction that high-spatial scoring students would also score high on ESP. The difference between high- and low-spatial scorers was significant (p = .0006). Explanations for scoring shift are offered.

238. Freeman, J. A. (1971). **Sex differences in precognition tests with seventh grade students** [Summary]. *Proceedings of the Parapsychological Association*, *8*, 63-65.

Four seventh-grade classes were tested for precognition, using a special test booklet with rows of words and symbols, alternately different and the same. Two classes scored significantly on word trials ($p < .01$ and $p < .03$), one class scored at chance, and one had results (p - .01) opposite to the prediction that girls would score above chance on rows of "same" symbol and "same" word and boys would do the reverse. Additional analyses of data are presented.

239. Freeman, J. A. (1971). **Sex differences in an ESP test.** *Journal of Parapsychology*, *35*, 58-59.

A ten-page ESP booklet was given to four seventh-grade classes along with two subtests of the Primary Mental Abilities test (PMA). PMA scores were not useful in differentiating between positive and negative ESP scoring of students. Girls scored higher than boys on rows of same symbol and different words. Boys scored the reverse. Two classes scored significantly in the expected direction, one scored in the opposite direction, and one scored at chance. Word trials contributed to most of the significance ($p < .001$).

240. Honorton, C. (1967). **Creativity and precognition scoring level.** Journal of Parapsychology, 31, 29-42.

Twenty-six junior high schoolers were given the Unusual Question test, Torrence's Creative Motivation Inventory, and a precognitive test using Zener cards. Significant correlations were found between ESP scores and the Unusual Question test scores and between scores on the Creative Motivation Inventory and the Unusual Question test. Another five series with additional creativity tests was conducted with a total of 276 high schoolers (ages 15-18) and 29 junior high schoolers (ages 12-14). The total of 305 students had 2,550 precognitive runs, resulting in overall nonsignificant ($p = .10$) psi-missing. Additional analyses were conducted with the additional creative tests given.

C. High schoolers (15-17 years)

241. Carpenter, J. C. (1971). **An attempt at using mood-variance relationships in effecting a "psi-transmission."** Journal of Parapsychology, 35, 57.

Seventeen high school students completed five sittings of five 24-trial precognitive runs. Targets were a circle and a cross. In addition, a Mood Adjective Check List was used. Statistically significant results showed that 10 out of 12 "message" items in the target list were correctly identified.

242. Carpenter, J. C. (1983). **Prediction of forced-choice ESP performance: I. A mood-adjective scale for predicting the variance of ESP run scores.** Journal of Parapsychology, 47, 191-216.

A total of 130 high school students participated in nine cross-validating precognition studies (10-12 subjects per experiment). A scale of mood items was generated for the prediction of run-score variance (RSV) in the forced-choice ESP task. A positive finding was that the scale proved reliable in predicting RSV for subjects relatively low in authoritarian tendencies.

243. Freeman, J. A. (1964). **A precognition test with a high-school science club.** Journal of Parapsychology, 28, 214-221.

Forty high school students (22 girls, 18 boys) took part in a group precognitive test by listing like or dislike in one of five blanks (one of which was later chosen as the target position) beside words on a list. Statistically significant results showed those with higher liked words showed a positive deviation on ESP targets associated with liked words. Also found was a negative deviation on ESP target position associated with disliked words found. The converse was also found to be statistically significant.

244. Freeman, J. A. (1966). **Sex differences and target arrangement: High school booklet tests of precognition.** Journal of Parapsychology, 30, 227-235.

A precognition task using a 10-page booklet had targets (symbols, words) arranged in rows containing alike and different targets. The pilot study with 15 girls and 18 boys showed girls scoring higher when rows contained different symbols and same words. Boys scored reversed. Results of four confirmatory studies (with a total of 96 junior high and high schoolers) had scores in the expected direction. The difference between total predicted positive and negative results was statistically significant ($p = .0008$).

245. Freeman, J. A. (1959). **The psi-differentiated effect in a precognition test.** Journal of Parapsychology, 33, 206-212.

Twenty high schoolers were separated into likers (L) and dislikers (D) on the basis of responses on the Freeman Word Reaction Test. A target position was chosen for each L or D and student's attempts to select correct positions constituted a precognitive hit or miss. It was expected that students would score positively on placement of primary responses and negatively on placement of secondary responses. Results were in the expected direction.

246. Freeman, J. A. (1970). **Mood, personality, and attitude in precognition tests.** Journal of Parapsychology, 34, 226.

Seventeen high schoolers were classified as Likers and Dislikers from responses on the Freeman Word-Reaction Test. Aside from the precognitive test, they were also given the Eysenck Personality Inventory (EPI) and Nielsen Mood Scale. High-neurotic-extreme-mood students and low-neurotic-moderate-mood students gave better results than high-neurotic-moderate-mood and low-neurotic-moderate-mood students. There was a significant difference between the first two groups ($p < .0009$). The second two groups scored insignificantly and in a direction opposite to that which was expected.

247. Freeman, J. A. (1970). **ESP performance before a TV camera.** Journal of Parapsychology, 34, 274-275.

ESP booklet tests were administered in conjunction with verbal and spatial sections of the Primal Mental Abilities test, as part of a program being filmed for TV. The predicted significant difference between positive and negative runs ($p < .01$) was found.

248. Hearne, K. M. T. (1982). **An ostensible precognition of the accidental sinking of H.M. Submarine Artemis in 1971.** Journal of the Society for Psychical Research, 51, 283-287.

A 17-year-old girl dreamt of the sinking of a submarine and subsequent entrapment of three sailors two weeks prior to the event in 1971. Details of the subject's life history and a personality profile are given.

249. Kanthamani, H. & Rao, H. H. (1975). **Response tendencies and stimulus structure.** Journal of Parapsychology, 39, 97-105.

Three series of group precognitive tests with high schoolers were conducted. The ESP task consisted of selecting which three-syllable word (one meaningful and two meaningless words per column) would be selected later as the target. The first series (32 students) showed psi-missing. The next two series (26 and 38 students) had average scores higher than chance. The difference between groups was significant ($p < .01$).

250. Neilsen, W. (1970). **Group targets, mood and personality characteristics -- a second study.** Journal of Parapsychology, 34, 229-230.

Nineteen high school students were given three 25-trial precognitive runs and the Eysenck Personality Inventory. As in an earlier experiment, high-neurotic students scored higher on the group target than low-neurotic students ($p < :005$). No significant difference was found between high-extroversion and low-extroversion groups.

251. Nielsen, W. (1970). **Possible relationship of precognition and creativity.** Journal of Parapsychology, 34, 281.

Gifted high schoolers (40) were given the Welsh Revised Art Scale (RA), a mood scale, the Eysenck Personality Inventory, and a precognitive test. Half of the subjects were given a five-choice ESP test, with the remainder of subjects given a two-choice task. Results showed no overall relationship between RA creativity and precognitive scores. There was significant scoring between type of ESP task and creative/noncreative response to the RA ($p < .01$). When mood and introversion/extroversion were considered, significance rose to $p < .001$. The results suggest five-choice tasks may produce more significant differential effects than two-choice tasks.

252. Schmidt, H. (1970). **Precognition test with a high school group.** Journal of Parapsychology, 34, 70.

A precognition test using an electronic four-choice machine was given individually to 19 high schoolers who had listened to a talk on ESP. A total of 648 trials resulted in 132 hits, 30 less than chance for a significant psi-missing score of $p < .005$. A second task encouraged psi-missing, with a total of 126 trials performed, resulting in 44. Significant psi-missing resulted at $p < .005$.

253. Winkelman, M. (1981). **The effect of formal education on extrasensory abilities: The Ozolco Study.** Journal of Parapsychology, 45, 321-336.

Three experiments assessed whether or not an increase in formal education inhibits ESP abilities. Subjects were 29 children from a rural Mexican village (ages 8-14), with zero to seven years of education. Clairvoyance testing with candy yielded significant results ($p < .005$), while use of marbles in clairvoyance testing was nonsignificant. Precognitive testing with candy was significant at the .05 level, while precognition testing using marbles was nonsignificant. PK testing using marbles yielded $p < .1$. There were no strong significant differences between males and females. Additional testing of field independence, conservation, math, and years of schooling were correlated. Total ESP correlated negatively with math ($p < .02$), schooling ($p < .03$), conservation, field independence, and age. Similar negative correlations were found with clairvoyance and precognition testing. PK correlated positively with age ($p < .006$).

254. Wood-Trost, L. (1981). **Possible precognition of the Teton Dam disaster in Idaho.** Journal of the Society for Psychical Research, 51, 65-74.

Reports are given from 13 females and 5 males (ages 15 to 76) of their precognitive perceptions of the collapse of the Teton Dam in 1976.

Article

255. Peterson, J. (1975). **Extrasensory abilities of children: An ignored reality?** Journal of Learning, 11-14.

The author criticizes the field of parapsychology for not conducting research on children and clairvoyant vision. As a camp counselor, the author recounts experiences reported by eight- and nine-year-old boys who saw colored lights coming out of the author's body. He urges openness, sensitivity to, and an understanding of reports from children without condemning their comments.

IV. PSYCHOKINESIS

IV. PSYCHOKINESIS

256. Bender, H., Vandrey, R., & Wendlandt, S. (1976). **"The Geller effect" in western Germany and Switzerland: A preliminary report on a social and experimental study** [Summary]. In J. D. Morris, W. G. Roll, & R. L. Morris (Eds.), Research in Parapsychology 1975 (pp. 141-144). Metuchen, NJ: Scarecrow Press.

This summarizes encounters with some youths who claimed to be able to bend metal objects repeatedly, mainly spoons. Results of experimental work with an 11-year-old boy having supposed PK abilities are also included.

257. Bierman, D. J. (1983). **Exploring the fundamental hypothesis of the observational theories using a PK test for babies** [Summary]. In W. G. Roll, J. Beloff, & R. A. White (Eds.), Research in Parapsychology 1982 (p. 97). Metuchen, NJ: Scarecrow Press.

Two 10-month-old babies were tested for PK using a computer-controlled Random Number Generator. A nonsense block-pattern display was replaced by a laughing-face display and melody during a hit. On even-numbered trials, the hits were only counted, with no feedback given. Results of the 24 sessions resulted in overall missing in the prerecorded condition (nonsignificant).

258. Bierman, D. J. (1985). **A retro and direct PK test for babies with the manipulation of feedback: A first trial of independent replication using software exchange.** European Journal of Parapsychology, 5, 373-390.

Two 10-month-old infants were tested for PK abilities, using 24 runs on a high-speed RNG connected to a microcomputer. Prior to the session a target number was prerecorded into the computer. The session entailed instantaneously generated numbers and prerecorded numbers being compared with the target numbers. A hit resulted in the replacement for a few seconds of the original nonsense block pattern with a laughing-face display and melody. A no-feedback condition occurred on even-number trials. A second experiment with one 10-month-old was also conducted. Both experiments resulted in nonsignificant results in the feedback condition. A "skeptic" was sent the computer experiment and obtained significant hitting in the feedback condition.

259. Blackmore, S. & Troscianko, T. (1985). **Belief in the paranormal: Probability judgments, illusory control, and the 'chance baseline shift.'** British Journal of Psychology, 76, 459-468.

The authors hypothesize possible reasons for belief in the paranormal: 1) some belief in psi occurs from misjudgments of probability, and 2) some belief in psi comes from an illusion of control. Experiment I: Computer-controlled probability tasks with 50 females (ages 14-18) resulted in sheep performing worse than goats on most tasks and significantly worse at responding appropriately to sample-size changes. Experiment II: The results with college subjects showed that sheep were significantly worse at questions involving sampling. Experiment III: This utilized a computer-controlled coin-toss task. While college sheep subjects felt that they had exercised greater control than goats, they estimated that they had fewer hits. No evidence of psi was found in all three experiments.

260. Bononcini, A. & Martelli, A. (1983). **Psychological investigation of subjects who are protagonists of alleged PK phenomena: A preliminary report.** Journal of the Society for Psychical Research, 52, 117-125.

Psychological tests were administered to four boys who demonstrated spontaneous PK phenomena, ages 10, 14, 8, and 15 when the phenomena first occurred. The first three were "mini-Gellers": the last was the focus of a poltergeist case. The authors conclude that any model of PK phenomena relating them to the central nervous system should also consider some subjects who appear normal.

261. Braud, W. (1981). **Psychokinesis experiments with infants and young children** [Summary]. In W. G. Roll & J. Beloff (Eds.), Research in Parapsychology 1980, (pp. 30-31). Metuchen, NJ: Scarecrow Press.

Experiment I: Subjects were four male and five female chilren (ages 4-6) tested on a binary random generator for movement of a remote-controlled toy truck. Nonsignificant results were obtained. Experiment II: Ten male and eight female children (ages 7-8) had to move the toy truck. The first run resulted in significant hitting ($p = .039$); the second run was nonsignificant. Experiment III: This involved time-displaced PK using infants six weeks to 12 months, with the playback of the mother's voice as feedback. The results approached significance.

262. Delanoy, D. (1987). **Work with a fraudulent PK metal-bending subject.** Journal of the Society for Psychical Research, 54, 247-256. Reprinted in D. H. Weiner & R. L. Morris (Eds.), Research in Parapsychology 1987 (pp. 102-105). Metuchen, NJ: Scarecrow Press.

A male (age 17) self-alleged PK subject participated in 20 sessions over seven months. The work covered micro-PK, macro-PK, fire-raising, and Ganzfeld. Evidence was obtained that showed blatantly fraudulent activities. The article raises concerns over intentional and unintentional deception in research.

263. Egely, G. (1986). **A pilot study of PK on liquids** [Summary]. In D. Weiner & D. Radin (Eds.), Research in Parapsychology 1985 (pp. 62-66). Metuchen, NJ: Scarecrow Press.

Secondary school students, (301 total subjects; ages 14-17) attempted to use PK to induce movement in fluid contained in a petri dish under a glass box. Movies of the sessions were also made. Out of 353 controlled test runs, one-third contained no noticeable movement. In the remaining two-thirds, movements were usually tangential, starting counter-clockwise, then turning to a steady clockwise movement relatively quickly. Article also appears as Egely, G. (1985). **PK research in Hungary: A pilot study of ostensible PK on liquids.** PSI Research, 4, 32-44.

264. Ellison, A. J. (1977). **Some problems in testing "mini-Gellers"** [Summary]. In J. D. Morris, W. G. Roll, & R. L. Morris (Eds.), Research in Parapsychology 1976 (pp. 203-206). Metuchen, NJ: Scarecrow Press.

This discusses difficulties encountered in testing a 13-year-old boy and his 11-year-old sister for PK, at their home and in the laboratory. Lab experiments showed few positive results. It was felt that the newly developed experimental techniques used to measure small physical quantities often lead to artifacts and should be pretested on a non-psi group first. "Laboratory inhibition" should be expected and allowed for. Experiments which can be done in familiar surroundings or in the subject's own home are best.

265. Giesler, P. V. (1985). **An attempted replication of Winkelman's ESP and socialization research** [Summary]. In R. A. White & J. Solfvin (Eds.) Research in Parapsychology 1984 (pp. 24-27). Metuchen, NJ: Scarecrow Press.

Thirty-six children living in Brazil (18 males, 18 females; ages 8-16) were given 30 trials of a clairvoyance (CV) task, 40 PK trials, and a formal math test with educational years controlled. The CV test involved guessing which of three colored candy balls out of nine total would be selected; the reward given was a similar candy from a different bag. The PK task required influencing a random-event generator to light either one of two light bulbs on its machine, with one series having a small statue of a regional deity behind one bulb. Overall PK and CV scores were negative and nonsignificant, thus not confirming Winkelman's results. CV, PK, and math correlations were nonsignificant.

266. Hasted, J. B. (1976). **An experimental study of the validity of metal bending phenomena.** Journal of the Society for Psychical Research, 48, 365-383.

Ten children (6 boys, four girls; ages 7-17) were tested, as well as Uri Geller. Field work conducted in the children's homes is reported. Also supplied is a discussion on methods of trickery that can be used to simulate PK. The article summarizes methods and equipment used, as well as various PK effects on different metals. A paperclip, usually of nickel-plated steel, was found most suitable for PK experiments with children.

267. Hasted, J. B. (1977). **Physical aspects of paranormal metal bending.** Journal of the Society for Psychical Research, 49, 583-607.

PK metal bending experiments were conducted over 13 days with a 17-year-old boy, using strain-gauge sensors.

Experiments took place in the subject's home. Metal bending did occur, and the author offers extensive documentation of the events.

268. Hasted, J. B. & Robertson, D. (1980). **Paranormal action on metal and its surroundings.** Journal of the Society for Psychical Research, 50, 379-398.

This article analyzes the dynamic strain data obtained from the effects of child paranormal metal bending; the strips of metal were suspended beyond their reach. Psychological, electrical, and structural effects are also considered.

269. Jacobs, J. C., Michels, J. A. G., Verbraak, A. (1978). **An experimental study on the influence of experimenter's expectancies on life span age differences in PK-performance.** European Journal of Parapsychology, 2, 213-227.

Subjects in three age categories were tested with dice for PK: children (age 5 maximum), adults (age 15 minimum; 35 maximum), and retired (age 65 minimum). Each category had 108 subjects within it. Each of six experimenters working with the subjects was told to expect that one of the age categories would have better PK, so that experimenter expectations varied. Although it was hypothesized that subjects' scores would be in accordance with experimenters' expectations about age, this was not confirmed; however, the unexpected result emerged of adult and retired females scoring higher than adult and retired males.

270. Kasahara, T., Kohri, N., Ro, Y., Imai, S., & Otani, S. (1981). **A study on PK ability of a gifted subject in Japan** [Summary]. In W. G. Roll & J. Beloff (Eds.), Research in Parapsychology 1980 (pp. 39-42). Metuchen, NJ: Scarecrow Press.

PK experiments with a 17-year-old male involved spoon bending and thoughtography under various conditions. Corollary physiological recordings were also made. Indications of PK were noted but conditions were not tamper-proof.

271. Keil, J. & Osborne, C. (1981). **Recent cases in Australia suggestive of directly observable PK** [Summary]. In W. G. Roll & J. Beloff (Eds.), Research in Parapsychology 1980, (pp. 35-39). Metuchen, NJ: Scarecrow Press.

Three subjects ages (2 males, 1 female; ages 15-17) were observed obtaining 360 degree movements of dumbbells suspended in a perspex cover under a Faraday cage.

272. McMahan, E. (1945). **PK experiments with two-sided objects.** Journal of Parapsychology, 9, 249-263.

Two experiments are reported in which two-sided objects are used with chutes and a revolving tube, instead of the usual rolling of dice, to test the PK hypothesis. Subjects were mostly college students tested individually for 26 sessions, with 1,300 runs yielding nonsignificant results. For the second experiment, using plastic discs, children (ages 5-11), adolescent girls, and adolescents/young adults (ages 16-20) were tested in groups of six to seven people. Each had two turns. The first run gave significantly high scores, the second significantly low scores. There was a significant difference between the rate of scoring on the first and second runs. Rewards of candy, toys, and movie tickets were offered.

273. McMahan, E. (1946). **A PK experiment with discs.** Journal of Parapsychology, 10, 169-180.

Subjects were adolescent girls and girls (ages 5-11), divided into four groups of six to seven, tested within a social setting. In a session, each girl was given three trials at the rotating cage apparatus. A nonsignificant decline was noted throughout the three trials. A significant decline in the distribution of hits within each trial was seen, with a significant difference between upper left and lower right quarters. These results, combined with the previously mentioned experiment (McMahan 1945), form significant findings. Quarter distribution given by the discs is similar to the distribution from the use of discs in PK experiments. Prizes of toys, candy, and movie tickets were given.

274. McMahan, E. (1947). **A PK experiment under light and dark conditions.** Journal of Parapsychology, 11, 46-54.

A PK disc experiment with girls (ages 5-11) and adolescent girls was conducted in a social atmosphere under light and dark conditions. A positive deviation was obtained under dark conditions and a negative deviation under the light. The difference in scoring between the two conditions gave a suggestive, though nonsignificant, probability of .014. The novelty effect of darkness is offered as a probable explanation for the scoring trends.

275. Nianlin, Z., Tianmin, Z., Xin, L., & Jun, M. (1983). **The primary measurements of mechanical effects of paranormal ability of human beings.** PSI Research, 2, 25-30.

A gifted 12-year-old girl moved the hands of a watch using psychokinesis. Five additional subjects were subsequently trained. Oscilloscope and cameras were used to detect fraud. The authors concluded that psychic forces were used, generating individual pulses of a power of more than 100 milliwatts.

276. Noville Pauli, E. (1976). **El poder de la mente sobre objetivos vivientes en funcion del sexo de las sujetos. [The power of mind over living targets as a function of sex of subjects.]** Psi Comunicacion, 2, 53-60.

Studies used children and youngsters as subjects to see if PK could influence wheat seed growth. Three seed groups (control, seeds for males, seeds for females) were used. There was more growth for males than for females and no significant results with groups formed of males and females vs. control.

277. Price, E. A. (1977). **The investigation of "mini-Gellers" in South Africa 18 months after their manifestation** [Summary]. In J. D. Morris, W. G. Roll, & R. L. Morris (Eds.), Research in Parapsychology 1976 (pp. 18-20). Metuchen, NJ: Scarecrow Press.

Six children and three adolescents, out of 137 claiming ability to bend metal objects, were investigated. Two successfully bent spoons under observation. Four were able to bend metal objects they could stroke and actually broke metal, as well as bent and broke plastic objects. No one bent copper or steel strips sealed within glass tubes.

278. Randall, J. L. (1974). **An extended series of ESP and PK tests with three English schoolboys.** Journal of the Society for Psychical Research, 47, 485-494.

Extended ESP and PK tests were conducted with three high schoolers who had previously done well in classroom ESP tests. Two subjects repeated their original performance in the predicted direction with significant scores. Each subject also did PK tests moving a gerbil to the left or right side of a box. One subject scored significantly ($p < .036$). Subjects also did PK with a binary random number generator, but results were not significant. One subject's data showed a chronological decline that was statistically significant ($p < .025$).

279. Randall, J. L. & Davis, C. P. (1982). **Paranormal deformation of nitinol wire: A confirmatory experiment.** Journal of the Society for Psychical Research, 51, 368-373.

Over a two-year period, an 11-year-old boy was tested for PK ability in bending metal strips and thick wires. The subject was successful in altering the permanent memory of a nitinol wire. Results confirmed previous research carried out by Dr. Byrd with Uri Geller.

280. Schmidt, H. & Pantas, L. (1972). **Psi tests with internally different machines.** Journal of Parapsychology, 36, 222-232.

A large group of subjects from elementary school age to adult were individually tested within a group setting. A specially constructed machine preselected one of four target lights according to an internal electronic target generator for the precognitive trials. By the subject's flipping a switch, a hit was achieved through the subject's mental activation of the internally selected target (PK). Results were statistically significant within each of the two trials but showed no significant difference between the scores of the two trials. A second experiment testing a single high scorer showed similar results.

281. Shafer, M. G. (1981). **PK metal bending in a semi-formal small group** [Summary]. In W. G. Roll & J. Beloff (Eds.), Research in Parapsychology 1980 (pp. 32-35). Metuchen, NJ: Scarecrow Press.

Described are two years' exploratory research in PK metal bending conducted with 13 subjects (ages 12-40; 5 were under 20). All subjects claimed to be able to bend stainless steel spoons or other cutlery. A variety of conditions and situations were set up. Results, although inconclusive, indicated that macro-PK influences were exerted on some occasions.

282. Tart, C. T. & Palmer, J. (1979). **Some psi experiments with Matthew Manning.** Journal of the Society for Psychical Research, 50, 224-228.

Three PK experiments involving the influencing of a spinning coin to fall heads or tails, forced choice random number guessing, and seeing auras, were conducted with a teenage boy with apparent psi abilities.

283. Terry, J. & Schmidt, H. (1978). **Conscious and subconscious PK tests with pre-recorded targets** [Summary]. In W. G. Roll (Ed.), Research in Parapsychology 1977 (pp. 36-41). Metuchen, NJ: Scarecrow Press.

Volunteers (ages 15-81) were each given six runs (each lasting 4 1/2 minutes. Three runs tested for "subconscious PK," alternating with three "conscious PK" runs. Results confirm the existence of a PK effect when the subjects made conscious PK effort. There was significant PK missing (p < .005) and a significantly high variance (p < .005).

284. Vasse, P. & Vasse, C. (1955). **PK and ESP experiments with Martie Vasse.** In Proceedings of the First International Conference of Parapsychological Studies (pp. 27-29). NY: Parapsychology Foundation, Inc.

This describes continuing ESP and PK experiments with the authors' daughter (age 3 1/2). Results showed that when ESP was high, PK was also high. There were 39 ESP runs yielding 264 hits (chance is 195), and 78 PK runs with 381 hits (chance is 312).

285. Weiner, D. H., Haight, J. M., Marion, M. D., & Munson, R. J. (1980). **The possible value of repeated visitation in group testing** [Summary]. In W. G. Roll (Ed.), Research in Parapsychology 1979 (pp. 177-179). Metuchen, NJ: Scarecrow Press.

This summarizes a study done in an elementary school mini-group teaching situation, with nine fifth and sixth graders in group one (5 males; 4 females) and ten fourth and fifth graders in group two (6 males; 4 females). There was informal competition between boys and girls in all tasks. Session one was precognition, using a random number generator. Results were nonsignificant. Session two was macro-PK, where boys and girls tried to influence the growth of rye seeds on separate trays. Pooled results were significant at $p < .05$. Session three was precognitive, using a random number generator, with prizes to the highest scorer of the group. Boys scored above chance and girls below in group one ($p < .05$); this was reversed in group two ($p < .01$). The authors conclude that repeated visitation combined with prizes can be a successful procedure.

286. Weiner, D. H. & Munson, R. J. (1981). **"The importance of repeated visitation in group testing: A disconfirmation."** Journal of Parapsychology, 45, 155-156.

This is an attempted replication of a previous study (see Weiner, et al., 1980). Group one (5 males; 5 females) had one third grader, four fourth graders, and five fifth graders. Group two consisted entirely of sixth graders. All tests again employed competition between the sexes. In session one, PK with a random number generator, there was an overall difference between boys' and girls' performance ($p < .05$). In session two, where students influenced rye-seed sprout lengths, results were not significant. The authors conclude that variables other than familiarity, such as contact with two experimenters of the opposite sex, affected the scores in the first study.

287. Winkelman, M. (1981). **The effects of schooling and formal education upon extrasensory abilities** [Summary]. In W. G. Roll & J. Beloff (Eds.), Research in Parapsychology 1980 (pp. 26-29). Metuchen, NJ: Scarecrow Press.

In Mexico, clairvoyance and PK tests were performed on an evenly divided group of 40 children (ages 7-14). A variety of clairvoyance tests included 20 trials using three colors of gum, marbles, and crayons. PK tests involved the use of marbles and dice. Additional educational tests were given (math, reading, memory, and Children's Embedded Figures Test). Clairvoyance tests showed no individual or overall significance. PK with marbles was nonsignificant, while PK with dice was positively significant ($p < .05$). Negative correlations with schooling, ages, and clairvoyance were significant.

288. Winkelman, M. (1981). **The effect of formal education on extrasensory abilities: The Ozolco Study.** Journal of Parapsychology, 45, 321-336.

Three experiments assessed whether or not an increase in education inhibits ESP abilities. Subjects were 29 children from a rural Mexican village (ages 8-14), with zero to seven years of education. Clairvoyance testing with candy yielded significant results ($p < .005$) while use of marbles in clairvoyance testing was nonsignificant. Precognitive testing with candy was significant at the .05 level, while precognition using marbles was nonsignificant. PK testing using marbles yielded $p < .1$. There were no strong significant differences between males and females. Additional testing of field independence, conservation, math, and years of schooling were correlated. Total ESP correlated negatively with math ($p < .02$), schooling ($p < .03$), conservation, field independence, and age. Similar negative correlations were found with clairvoyance and precognition testing. PK correlated positively with age ($p < .006$).

Article

289. Taylor, J. (1975). **The spoon benders.** Psychic, 6(5), 8-12.

The article reviews cases of children who are able to mentally bend spoons and other metal items. It also discusses Uri Geller's PK metal-bending abilities.

V. POLTERGEISTS

V. POLTERGEISTS

290. Barrett, W. F. (1911). **Poltergeists, old and new.** Proceedings of the Society for Psychical Research, 25, 377-412.

This discusses previously unpublished accounts involving poltergeist phenomena from 1868-1910. Many cases involve young children (ages 11-15). It also briefly summarizes when and where phenomena occur, as well as the duration and age range.

291. Eisler, W. (1975). **The Bronx poltergeist** [Summary]. In J. D. Morris, W. G. Roll, & R. L. Morris (Eds.), Research in Parapsychology 1974 (pp. 139-143). Metuchen, NJ: Scarecrow Press.

This summarizes an investigation of a poltergeist case involving a Bronx family. Phenomena center around an adopted daughter (age 8 1/2). Ninety-four events witnessed by family and neighbors occurred over a one-month period; 43 events took place while the investigator was at the house for six days. Events occurred only when the child was at home, and objects generally moved toward the girl rather than away.

292. Gregory, A. (1982). **London experiments with Matthew Manning.** Proceedings of the Society for Psychical Research, 56, 284-366.

This examines poltergeist activity in an English family's home and discusses the young adult son's personality and automatic-writing experiences. Psi experiments conducted with him are described in detail.

293. Jacobs, J. C., Michels, J. A. G., Verbraak, A. (1978). **An experimental study on the influence of experimenter's expectancies on life span age differences in PK-performance.** European Journal of Parapsychology, 2, 213-227.

Subjects in three age categories were tested with dice for PK: children (age 5 maximum), adults (age 15 minimum, 35 maximum), and retired (age 65 minimum). Each category working with the subjects was told to expect that one of the age categories would have better PK, so that experimenter expectations varied. Although it was hypothesized that subjects' scores would be in accordance with experimenters' expectations about age, this was not confirmed; however, the unexpected result emerged of adult and retired females scoring higher than adult and retired males.

294. Lang, A. (1904). **The poltergeist at Cideville.** Proceedings of the Society for Psychical Research, 18, 454-463.

The case of the Presbyters of Cideville (1850-51) is summarized from Dale Owen's writing Footfalls on the Boundary of Another World (London, 1861, pp. 195-203). Documents of what almost appears to be an 1851 witchcraft trial were obtained by the SPR. The case involves two boys (ages 12 and 14) with various phenomena occurring: raps, shovels and tongs moved and then returned to the same spot, table and chairs spun around, and knives flung about.

295. Lawden, D. F. (1979). **On a poltergeist case.** Journal of the Society for Psychical Research, 50, 73-76.

Poltergeist-like activity over a six-month period involving a 17-year-old girl is reported.

296. Lucadou, W. (1981). **Report about a recent alleged RSPK case in Frankfurt** [Summary]. In W. G. Roll & J. Beloff (Eds.), Research in Parapsychology 1980 (pp. 58-60). Metuchen, NJ: Scarecrow Press.

RSPK phenomena (stone throwing) allegedly occurred in a family of six, with the 14-year-old daughter the likely originator of the phenomena.

297. Martinez-Taboas, A. (1984). **An appraisal of the role of aggression and the central nervous system in RSPK agents.** Journal of the American Society for Psychical Research, 78, 55-69.

The author examines and criticizes the common practices of associating repressed aggression and/or CNS disturbances with RSPK agents. He states that the psychological evaluations used have not been administered under blind conditions, and unreliable projective tests have been used. The CNS theory is criticized as not being testable. Alternative tests are proposed.

298. Mathews, F. M. & Solfvin, G. F. (1977). **A case of RSPK in Massachusetts: Part I - poltergeist** [Summary]. In J. D. Morris, W. G. Roll, & R. L. Morris (Eds.), Research in Parapsychology 1976 (pp. 219-223). Metuchen, NJ: Scarecrow Press.

This reports the case of a woman (age 67) and three great-grandsons, one preschool age, the others seven and nine years old. Physical events were viewed by the observer, though none were obtained on film or EEG. Authors believe incidents were induced as a vicarious form of revenge by the children. During six weeks of observation, 184 incidents were reported. These disturbances had also occurred prior to present tenants, and the investigators suggest that a haunting may have triggered the poltergeist activity.

299. O'Connor, K. (1978). **Poltergeists: Are they really spirits?** New England Journal of Parapsychology, 1, 44-52.

This is a generally good overview and summary of the literature and findings within the field of poltergeist research. A case study written in the format of a young boy's narrative is included. Various theories around the events are explored.

300. Palmer, J. (1974). **A case of RSPK involving a 10 year old boy: The Powhatan Poltergeist.** Journal of the American Society for Psychical Research, 68, 1-33.

A ten-year-old black boy living with elderly foster parents in the rural southern U.S. appeared to be the center of poltergeist activity. Over 50 incidents were reported by 11 eyewitnesses, all interviewed within two weeks of the events. The investigator did not witness any convincing phenomena. Most movements occurred within five feet of the boy. Patterns included statistically significant tendencies for objects to move toward the boy as opposed to away from him, from behind him when walking, and from in front when stationary. Repressed hostility toward the foster parents is suggested for the phenomena, with suggestions made for testing this general hypothesis in laboratory PK research. Neurological examination, including EEG, indicated no abnormalities.

301. Permutt, C. (1983). **The Bournemouth Poltergeist.** Journal of the Society for Psychical Research, 52, 45-51.

Events of activity are reported from an English home with a seventeen-year-old adopted daughter and an eight-year-old foster son. Reports were verified by a clergyman, social worker, and policeman who were witnesses. The author concludes that these events fall more into the RSPK category.

302. Pratt, J. G. (1978). **The Pearisburg poltergeist** [Summary]. In W. G. Roll (Ed.), Research in Parapsychology 1977 (pp. 174-182). Metuchen, NJ: Scarecrow Press.

This summarizes poltergeist events surrounding a nine-year-old foster child. Heavy shelves were turned over and items moved by themselves. The intensity and short duration of the main series of events appear as outstanding features of this case.

303. Pratt, J. G. & Palmer, J. (1976). **An investigation of an unpublicized family poltergeist** [Summary]. In J. D. Morris, W. G. Roll, & R. L. Morris (Eds.), Research in Parapsychology 1975 (pp. 109-114). Metuchen, NJ: Scarecrow Press.

This summarizes a poltergeist case involving a nine-year-old boy and a ten-year-old girl living with their grandparents. Events are discussed and analyzed. The authors conclude that some genuine RSPK existed, mixed with intentional trickery.

304. Pratt, J. G. & Roll, W. G. (1958). **The Seaford disturbances.** Journal of Parapsychology, 22, 79-124.

Poltergeist phenomena involving a 13-year-old girl and her 12-year-old brother are outlined. A complete listing of disturbances are arranged chronologically. Evidence is discussed in relation to three hypotheses other than PK: fraud, psychological aberrations, and purely physical causes. The authors consider that these three hypotheses do not satisfactorily explain the phenomena and consider the RSPK hypothesis worthy of consideration.

305. Rogo, D. S. (1982). **The poltergeist and family dynamics: A report on a recent investigation.** Journal of the Society for Psychical Research, 51, 233-237.

Recurrent spontaneous psychokinesis events were reported in the home of a sixteen-year-old girl and her parents. Psychological examinations (Rosenzweig Picture-Frustration Test, House-Tree-Person Test, and Rotter Incomplete Sentences Blank) were given to the teenager and her parents. Results indicated a family profile of a typical "poltergeist" personality and supported the author's view that RSPK phenomena are sometimes reactions of a total family to their situation, with not just one central agent.

306. Rogo, D. S. (1987). **A case of mysterious stone-throwing in Arizona.** Journal of the Society for Psychical Research, 54 16-37.

Stone-throwing poltergeist-like activity was witnessed by the author, who obtained interviews with other witnesses. Psychological and neurological testing of the family's four children revealed little information. A paranormal cause could neither be confirmed nor ruled out.

307. Roll, W. G. (1969). **The Newark disturbances.** Journal of the American Society for Psychical Research, 63, 123-174.

This summarizes an investigation of poltergeist disturbances surrounding a 13-year-old black boy living with his grandmother. The types of events that occurred and objects involved are described in detail, as are the results of a psychological examination of the boy. The case is compared to an earlier one investigated by Roll.

308. Roll, W. G. (1970). **Poltergeist phenomena and interpersonal relations.** Journal of the American Society for Psychical Research, 64, 66-99.

Over 110 disturbances occurred in the home of a 32-year-old woman, her 61-year-old mother, and her 13-year-old daughter. Personality and psychological tests were given to all. Results further confirmed indications that interpersonal relationships were characterized by frustration and anger. Most events appeared aimed at the grandmother, with the mother receiving a few physical injuries. The possibility of two agents is considered.

309. Roll, W. G. (1978). **Understanding the poltergeist** [Summary]. In W. G. Roll (Ed.), Research in Parapsychology 1977 (pp. 183-195). Metuchen, NJ: Scarecrow Press.

Roll analyzes 116 RSPK cases in depth, in terms of age, sex, health, and other factors relating to the focal persons, from incidents dating from 1849 to 1974. The age range of 45 involved females was from 12 to 19 years, with the age range of 31 males from 13 to 21 years.

310. Roll, W. G. (1984). **The psychopathological and psychophysiological theories of the RSPK agent** [Summary]. In R. A. White & R. Broughton (Eds.), Research in Parapsychology 1983 (pp. 118-119). Metuchen, NJ: Scarecrow Press.

This explores the question of whether or not there are CNS anomalies that can be linked to poltergeist phenomena. A survey of RSPK cases lends support to the CNS, pointing to probable epileptic seizure activity. The author postulates that RSPK-like epilepsy occurs primarily before age 15, and both RSPK incidents and epileptic symptoms are observed under stressful conditions.

311. Roll, W. G. & Montagno, E. deA. (1983). **Similarities between RSPK and psychomotor epilepsy** [Summary]. In W. G. Roll, J. Beloff, & R. A. White (Eds.), Research in Parapsychology 1982 (pp. 270-271). Metuchen, NJ: Scarecrow Press.

Several similar features are noted between RSPK and psychomotor epilepsy. Both peak in the early teens, involve equal proportions of males and females, consist of recurrent effects, are worldwide in distribution, involve displays of energy, are triggered spontaneously or in response to arousal, are associated with altered states of consciousness, and often express emotional states, notably violence.

312. Serecki-Wassilko, Z. (1927). **The early history and phenomena of Eleonore Zugun.** The British Journal of Psychical Research, 1, 133-150. (Reprinted as **Observations on Eleonore Zugun.** Journal of the American Society for Psychical Research, 1920, 20, 513-523 and 593-603.)

This recounts poltergeist phenomena in Rumania surrounding a 12-year-old girl near the time of her elderly grandmother's death. Objects flew about; the grandmother levitated to the ceiling and fell to the bed.

313. Solfvin, G. F. & Mathews, F. M. (1977). **A case of RSPK in Massachusetts: Part II - the haunting** [Summary]. In J. D. Morris, W. G. Roll, & R. L. Morris (Eds.), Research in Parapsychology 1976 (pp. 223-227). Metuchen, NJ: Scarecrow Press.

This summarizes a continuation of a poltergeist investigation involving three young boys ages seven, nine, and preschool, with possible haunting implications. (See Mathews, F. M. & Solfvin, G. F., 1977, cited previously.) The former tenants reported haunting occurrences, and the present tenant reported seeing apparitions and hearing noises. The authors concluded that the RSPK phenomena was initiated by the haunting.

314. Stevenson, I. (1972). **Are poltergeists living or are they dead?** Journal of the American Society for Psychical Research, 66, 233-251.

Two Asian poltergeist manifestations and cases from different cultures are discussed. In each of the three cases described, the principal subjects and/or informants attribute physical phenomena to disincarnate persons. In two cases, apparitional experiences occurred. The article concludes that some poltergeists are living and others are dead.

315. Stewart, J. L., Roll, W. G., & Baumann, S. (1987). **Hypnotic suggestion and RSPK** [Summary]. In D. H. Weiner & R. D. Nelson (Eds.), Research in Parapsychology 1986 (pp. 30-35). Metuchen, NJ: Scarecrow Press.

A female 15-year-old RSPK subject was hypnotized and participated in various experiments to generate RSPK events. Twenty-one incidents occurred while she was under observation. Eyewitness reports by researchers were given. However, no videotaping was obtained.

316. Zorab, G. (1964). **A further comparative analysis of some poltergeist phenomena: Cases from continental Europe.** Journal of the American Society for Psychical Research, 58, 105-127.

This recounts twenty varied cases involving families with children ranging in age from infancy to 18 years. The author reviews the similarities between cases, as well as discusses the possible underlying psychological factors determining the RSPK.

317. Zorab, G. (1973). **The Sitoebondo poltergeist.** Journal of the American Society for Psychical Research, 67, 391-406.

This discusses reports obtained from a photostat of a letter written in 1893 pertaining to poltergeist activity in Java, concerning a 13-year-old girl and her sister. Additional activity in other times and places, involving an eight-year-old and adolescent boys, among others, is mentioned. No events were witnessed by the author.

Books

318. Gauld, A. & Cornell, A. D. (1979). Poltergeists. London: Routledge and Kegan Paul.

This reviews 500 published poltergeist cases, in most of which the presumed agent was under 20 years old. Several new cases investigated by the authors, many involving children, are also reported. Various explanations for poltergeist disturbances, including trickery, recurrent spontaneous psychokinesis (RSPK), and intervention of the dead are considered. No single explanation seems to fit all cases.

319. Manning, M. (1974). The Link: The extraordinary gifts of a teenage psychic. London: Colin Smythe, Gerrards Cross; NY: Ballantine, 1976.

Written by the author when 18 years of age, the book gives supposedly true accounts of poltergeist phenomena occurring since he was age 11. These include automatic drawings from various renowned artists, messages written in different languages (most unknown to the author), and PK phenomena. Pictures and diagrams are supplied.

Reviewed by Fletcher, I. (1975). Journal of the Society for Psychical Research, 48, 104-106.

320. Owen, A. R. G. (1964). Can we explain the poltergeist? NY: Helix Press.

This investigates various possibilities for poltergeist events, including natural causes. There are several well-documented poltergeist cases involving young children (ages 11-16). Additional theories offered include biological, psychoneurotic, and mediumship.

Reviewed by Thouless, R. H. (1965). Journal of Parapsychology, 29, 207-209.

321. Roll, W. G. (1972). The Poltergeist. NY: Doubleday.

This includes clear and careful accounts of poltergeist phenomena with eyewitness reports, along with examples of various types of cases. Included is an in-depth discussion of two "poltergeist mediums." As long ago as 1851, children between 12-17 years are predominant in cases found around the world. Summary chapters try to explain each of the phenomena.

Reviewed by Owen, A. R. G. (1974). Journal of Parapsychology, 38, 94-97.

VI. REINCARNATION

VI. REINCARNATION

322. Barker, D. R. (1979). **What next in survival research: IV. From guesses to enumeration: Plans for a census of reincarnation type cases in India.** Journal of Indian Psychology, 2, 19-23.

A computerized analysis of 113 authenticated reincarnation cases yielded a typical profile of a case from North India. Among the factors are: around age 36 months of age the child speaks of a previous life, comes from a large family, is significantly low in birth order, has normal verbal and physical development, is preoccupied with past memories, displays behavior mimicking past life activities and tastes, has past life home approximately 20 kilometers away, has slight or indirect contact with this past life family, and has primary memories of previous life begin to fade at about age six, with normal development from six to eight years on.

323. Barker, D. R. & Pasricha, S. K. (1979). **Reincarnation cases in Fatehabad: A systematic survey in north India.** Journal of Asian and African Studies, 14, 230-240.

A survey of the Agra District in Uttar Pradesh, India, was conducted to determine: 1) the prevalence of reincarnation cases; 2) the characteristics of the sample cases; and 3) the diffusion of information about them. The prevalence of cases was found to be 2.2 cases per thousand. A total of 19 cases was found, all involving young children; in 13 cases a specific previous person had been identified as corresponding to the memories. Information about especially dramatic cases had spread beyond the survey district, but average cases were not known outside the village in which they occurred.

324. Chadha, N. & Stevenson, I. (1988). **Two correlates of violent death in cases of the reincarnation type.** Journal of the Society for Psychical Research, 55, 71-79.

In some cases of children who claimed to remember previous lives, the previous person died a natural death, whereas in other cases the death was violent. Data from 326 cases in eight different cultures were examined to see if there was a difference between the two types of cases. Violent death cases were found to have a shorter interval between the two lives ($p < .01$), with subjects who were younger when first speaking of the previous life ($p < .01$).

325. Chari, C. T. K. (1961-1962). **Parapsychology and "reincarnation." Part I.** Indian Journal of Parapsychology, 3(1), 20-31.

This reviews various aspects of reincarnation: criteria in judging cases, deja vu experiences, and evidence of birth marks. Chari mentions many reported cases of young children recalling past lives.

326. Chari, C. T. K. (1961-1962). **Parapsychology and "reincarnation." [Part II.] "Reincarnation or spirit possession?"** Indian Journal of Parapsychology, 3(2), 12-22.

Chari continues his critical review of reincarnation cases and urges further investigation. He suggests that "spiritual return" and "multiple personalities" should also be studied as extrasensorial cognition.

327. Chari, C. T. K. (1962). **Paramnesia and reincarnation.** Proceedings of the Society for Psychical Research, 53, 264-286.

Paramnesia refers to distortions of memory. Chari discusses deja vu, clinical and psychological theories of paramnesia, and hypotheses of telepathic and precognitive paramnesia, and shows how these may be used to explain apparent past life memories without recourse to reincarnation.

328. Chari, C. T. K. (1967). **Reincarnation: New light on an old doctrine.** International Journal of Parapsychology, 9, 217-222.

This is an essay review of Ian Stevenson's Twenty Cases Suggestive of Reincarnation. Chari acknowledges the quality of Stevenson's research, but he questions whether cultural factors are not enough to explain the cases, without recourse to the hypothesis of reincarnation.

329. Chari, C. T. K. (1981). **A new look at reincarnation.** Christian Parapsychologist, 4, 121-129.

Chari criticizes the "group characteristics" approach to reincarnation research, whereby weaknesses of individual cases are believed to be overcome by the common resemblance of all cases. The uneven geographical distribution of cases supports the idea that their true explanation lies in cultural factors. Some problematic Indian cases are described.

330. Cook, E. W., Pasricha, S., Samararatne, G., Maung, U W., & Stevenson, I. (1983). **A review and analysis of "unsolved" cases of the reincarnation type** [Summary]. In W. G. Roll, J. Beloff, & R. White (Eds.), Research in Parapsychology 1982 (pp. 214-217). Metuchen, NJ: Scarecrow Press.

General characteristics from the analysis of data of 856 reincarnation cases in six cultures are summarized. Unsolved cases are compared with solved ones in three important features: shorter duration of speaking about previous lives in unsolved cases ($p < .00001$), higher incidence of violent death in unsolved cases ($p < .00001$), and verified information in some unsolved cases. Unsolved cases range from 3% in Thailand to 80% in the U.S., with the lowest percentage unsolved in Burma, India, and Lebanon.

331. Cook, E. W., Pasricha, S., Samararatne, G., Maung, U W., & Stevenson, I. (1983). **A review and analysis of "unsolved" cases of the reincarnation type: I. Introduction and illustrative case reports.** Journal of the American Society for Psychical Research, 77, 45-62.

The importance of unsolved cases is discussed. Brief reports of seven unsolved cases in Lebanon, India, Burma, and Sri Lanka are given. The specificity of each child's statements seemed to indicate the need for a search, but in spite of inquiries, all are unsolved. Comments are offered as to why failure to verify may have occurred.

332. Cook, E. W., Pasricha, S., Samararatne, G., Maung, U W., & Stevenson, I. (1983). **A review and analysis of "unsolved" cases of the reincarnation type: II. Comparison of features of solved and unsolved cases.** Journal of the American Society for Psychical Research, 77, 115-135.

Analyses are given from 856 solved and unsolved reincarnation cases in six cultures. The highest proportion of solved cases are in Burma, Thailand, India, and Lebanon, with the lowest in Sri Lanka and the U.S. A statistically significant difference ($p < .00001$) was found between the ages when subjects stopped talking about the previous life, with unsolved cases occurring at 70 months vs. solved cases at 90 months. The subject mentioned the previous personality's name significantly more often in the solved cases than in the unsolved cases ($p < .00001$). In all cultures, there was a significantly higher ($p < .00001$) incidence of violent death among previous personalities in the unsolved cases.

333. Duxbury, E. W. (1930). **The problem of reincarnation.** Quarterly Transactions of the British College of Psychic Science, 91, 109-124.

This reports on the case of Dr. Carmelo Samona's twin daughters. The article is a translated account from a French work by M. Gabriel Delanne, "La Reincarnation." In 1910, the 5-year-old daughter of Samona died. She appeared to her mother in a dream, stating that she would be coming back. When a set of twin daughters was born, one had memories of the previous life of his daughter and looked identical to her. Documentation through friends' letters is offered in support.

334. Matlock, J. G. (1988). **Some further perspectives on reincarnation research: A rejoinder to D. Scott Rogo.** Journal of Religion and Psychical Research, 11, 63-70.

Rogo (1986) considered spontaneous past life memories of children and adults to be different types of experience, but it may be more appropriate to think of them as lying along a common continuum. Of 88 verified cases, the vast majority (82, or 93.2%) came from children under 5. In almost two thirds (61.3%) of the cases of this subgroup, the initial recall was entirely spontaneous. In the over-5 age group there was not a single instance of the initial memories occurring spontaneously in the waking state, although there were cases of memory occurring during meditation or dreaming. Matlock also addresses mistakes and misrepresentations in Rogo's discussion. (For correspondence related to this article, see Journal of Religion and Psychical Research, 11, 173-177.)

335. Matlock, J. G. (1989). **Age and stimulus in past life memory cases: A study of published cases.** Journal of the American Society for Psychical Research, 83, 303-316.

A total of 95 verified past life memory cases was analyzed for the relationship of the age of the subject, on first speaking of the previous life, to the presence or absence of a stimulus (cue) to the memories on that occasion. The median age of the 95 subjects was 2.75 years, and this was used to divide the sample into two age groups. The younger the child, the more likely the memories were to occur without stimulus both in all cases ($p = .00005$) and in a subseries of 30 Indian cases ($p = .0014$), tested by chi-squares. A two-factor ANOVA confirmed the relationship between age and stimulus, but found no significant difference between the two series on the interaction of variables.

336. Mills, A. C. (1988). **A comparison of Wet'suwet'en cases of the reincarnation type with Gitksan and Beaver.** Journal of Anthropological Research, 44, 385-416.

Past life memory cases of the Wet'suwet'en (Carrier) Indians of British Columbia are compared to cases from among the neighboring Gitksan and Beaver (see Mills, 1988). The Wet'suwet'en believe in neither changes of sex between lives nor the possibility of reincarnating in more than one child. Their cases also have an unusually long period between lives (median = 120 months), but otherwise are similar to those of the other groups.

337. Mills, A. C. (1988). **A preliminary investigation of cases of reincarnation among the Beaver and Gitksan Indians.** Anthropologica, 30, 23-59.

This compares child reincarnation cases from two Indian tribes in British Columbia. Birthmarks, behaviors, dreams, and statements that refer to previous lives figure in cases from both groups. However, the Beaver alone have cases of sex change between lives, and the Gitksan alone believe that the deceased may be reborn in more than one child. Some example cases are described.

338. Mills, A. C. (1989). **A replication study: Three cases of children in northern India who are said to remember a previous life.** Journal of Scientific Exploration, 3, 133-134.

The study reported here represents an effort by an independent investigator to research cases similar to those reported by I. Stevenson, using his methods. The three cases are chosen from ten investigated by the author. In one case the subject was only nine months old when she said the word "husband" and began to look for a picture of the man she remembered. In another case a child mimed limping even before he spoke about the life of a man who had limped. The third child began to speak about the previous life at 18 months. Mills describes many other details of these cases and discusses various interpretations of them, but ends by agreeing with Stevenson that reincarnation is the most satisfactory.

339. Mills, A. C. (1990). **Moslem cases of the reincarnation type in northern India: A test of the hypothesis of imposed identification. Part I: Analysis of 26 cases.** Journal of Scientific Exploration, 4, 171-188.

This discusses cases of Moslem and Hindu children who claim to remember previous lives. In eight cases, a Moslem child claimed to have been a Moslem, and in seven cases a Moslem child claimed to have been a Hindu. In eleven cases, a Hindu child claimed to have been a Moslem. The cases were similar in form and character to cases involving only Hindus. Because Moslems in India do not officially endorse the Hindu doctrine of reincarnation, and families of both religions were uncomfortable with the cases, the author argues that they cannot easily be explained in terms of imposed identification by the parents.

340. Mills, A. C. (1990). **Moslem cases of the reincarnation type in northern India: A test of the hypothesis of imposed identification. Part II: Reports of three cases.** Journal of Scientific Exploration, 4, 189-202.

Three Moslem and "half-Moslem" cases of children who claim to remember previous lives in India are described. In two of these cases, the previous personalities were identified. The third case remained unsolved, despite efforts to verify it, and may represent a spurious case.

341. Murphy, G. (1973). **A Caringtonian approach to Ian Stevenson's Twenty cases suggestive of reincarnation.** Journal of the American Society for Psychical Research, 67, 117-129.

Murphy applies the association theory of mind developed by Whately Carington to Stevenson's reincarnation data. The author suggests that much highly specific and personal material exists in reincarnation cases, which can be viewed in terms of persistence of an independent personal entity which leaves one body and "invades" another. However, there is also much that conflicts with this hypothesis. An alternative interpretation is suggested in terms of Carington psychon systems and psychometric linkages.

342. Pal, P. (1961-1962). **A case suggestive of reincarnation in West Bengal.** Indian Journal of Parapsychology, 3, 5-21.

A five-year-old child by the name of Sukla recounts memories of a previous life.

343. Pasricha, S. K. (1983). **New information favoring a paranormal interpretation in the case of Rakesh Gaur.** European Journal of Parapsychology, 5, 77-85.

This reports some additional findings from the author's investigation of a case originally reported with D. R. Barker (see Pasricha & Barker, 1981). The additional findings support the author's interpretation of the case as one of probable past life memory.

344. Pasricha, S. K. (1990). **Three conjectured features of reincarnation-type cases in north India: Responses of persons unfamiliar with actual cases.** Journal of the American Society for Psychical Research, 84, 227-233.

Persons with no direct acquaintance with children who claimed to remember previous lives were questioned on their beliefs about such cases, and their responses were compared to characteristics of actual cases. The respondents believed the children would be older both at first speaking about the previous life ($p < .001$) and at last speaking about it ($p < .001$) than data from actual cases suggest. However, the incidence of violent death in actual cases was not statistically different from the expectations of the informants.

345. Pasricha, S. K. & Barker, D. R. (1981). **A case of the reincarnation type in India: The case of Rakesh Gaur.** European Journal of Parapsychology, 3, 381-408.

This describes the case of a 5-year-old boy in northern India who claimed to remember a previous life. Although the previous person was identified, the boy's memories included several mistakes, and the authors reached different conclusions about whether the case involved paranormal cognition. (See also Pasricha, 1983.)

346. Pasricha, S. K. & Stevenson, I. (1977). **Three cases of the reincarnation type in India.** Indian Journal of Psychiatry, 19, 36-42.

This describes three cases of children who made veridical claims to remember previous lives. In one case, a girl began at 18 months to indicate the direction of the house she said she had lived in before, and later described in detail the life of a woman who had been murdered. In a second case, a girl was 3 and one half years old when she began to speak of the previous life, while in the third case the subject (a boy) was between 4 and 5 years old when he first began to relate his memories. Of particular interest are the pronounced behavioral features of these cases. Pasricha and Stevenson contrast them with cases diagnosed by Indian psychiatrists as ones of possession.

347. Pasricha, S. K. & Stevenson, I. (1979). **A partly independent replication of cases suggestive of reincarnation.** European Journal of Parapsychology, 3, 51-65.

Because children who say they remember previous lives normally stop speaking of their memories after a few years, independent replications of a given case are seldom possible. A different replication approach would involve the comparison of the features of different cases investigated by two or more persons. This paper reports the comparison of 45 cases investigated by Pasricha with 50 cases investigated by Stevenson. Statistically significant differences were found between the two series on 12 of 56 variables.

348. Pasricha, S. & Stevenson, I. (1987). **Indian cases of the reincarnation type two generations apart.** Journal of the Society for Psychical Research, 54, 239-246.

Comparisons were made between reincarnation cases of 36 subjects born before 1936 and 54 subjects born in 1965 or later. Out of 54 variables, significant differences were found for only five variables.

349. Prasad, J. & Stevenson, I. (1971). **Preliminary investigations of the correspondences in samskars (personality traits) of the present and previous personalities in cases of the reincarnation type in India** [Summary]. In W. G. Roll, R. L. Morris, & J. D. Morris (Eds.), Proceedings of the Parapsychological Association 1969, 6 (pp. 4-6). Durham, NC: Parapsychological Association.

Many children who claim to remember events of previous lives behave in ways that are odd for their families and peer groups but consistent with the personality and habits of the persons they talk about. This describes a questionnaire study designed to compare the personalities of the subjects and previous persons in six verified cases. Results are not presented. (See under **Books and Articles**, Prasad, 1973.)

350. Rankawat, B. D. (1959). **Study of spontaneous cases.** Indian Journal of Parapsychology, 1, 76-80.

This covers two investigations of reincarnation. The hypothesis of fraud and unconscious learning are ruled out by circumstantial evidence. The final decision is inconclusive, as the reincarnation incidents were reported much after their actual occurrences. The first case is of a seven-year-old boy who reportedly died at night at age three, but then recovered in a couple of days. During the same time, a 25-year-old was reported to have died due to an accident. The seven-year-old had memories of the other person's life and claimed he was this person. The second case was that of a six-year-old girl, who at age two and one-half reported having two houses and recounted information of another life. A brief report on nine-year-old twin girls is also included.

351. Rogo, D. S. (1986). **Researching the reincarnation question: Some current perspectives.** Journal of Religion and Psychical Research, 9, 128-137.

Rogo discusses reincarnation research under four headings: spontaneous past life memories of adults; "extracerebral memory" of children; hypnotic regression; and past life therapy. He is critical of some aspects of Stevenson's research with children. (See also Matlock, 1988.)

352. Roll, W. G. (1982). **Memory, mediumship, and reincarnation** [Summary]. In W. G. Roll, R. L. Morris, & R. A. White (Eds.), Research in Parapsychology 1981 (pp. 182-184). Metuchen, NJ: Scarecrow Press.

In cases of mediumship in which the communicator is unknown to either the medium or the sitters, the communicators usually lived in the same social or physical environment as those attending the seance. The same pattern appears in some reincarnation cases reported by Ian Stevenson. It also appears in some apparition cases, and may be due to the impression on the environment of a "memory" trace that is picked up by the subject. (See also Roll, W. G. (1983). **Errata.** In W. G. Roll, J. Beloff, & R. A. White (Eds.), Research in Parapsychology 1982, p. 336. Metuchen, NJ: Scarecrow Press.)

353. Stevenson, I. (1960). **The evidence for survival from claimed memories of former incarnations. Part I. Review of the data.** Journal of the American Society for Psychical Research, 54, 51-71.

The winning essay in a contest in honor of William James. Evidence is given for reincarnation through memories of former lives. Various hypotheses are offered along with descriptions of what evidence is viewed as relevant to reincarnation. Sensitives and mediums, along with the classification of various apparent memories, are discussed. In 44 cases, subjects, mostly children, claimed to remember the lives of persons who were found to have existed. Several cases are summarized: an eight-year-old Japanese boy, a French medium, a three-year-old girl from India, a four-year-old Cuban boy, a four-year-old boy from India, and a six-year-old Belgian boy.

354. Stevenson, I. (1960). **The evidence for survival from claimed memories of former incarnations. Part II. Analyses of the data and suggestions for further investigations.** Journal of the American Society for Psychical Research, 54, 95-117.

This discusses various hypotheses in evaluating data of apparent former life memories. Proposals are offered for further investigation and experimentation (through hypnosis).

355. Stevenson, I. (1960). **Criteria for the ideal case bearing on reincarnation.** Indian Journal of Parapsychology, 4, 149-155.

In an earlier paper (Stevenson, 1960), Stevenson reported having found 44 published cases of past life memory in which the previous person was identified. Since then he has become aware of several new cases, bringing the total number of cases to 75. The present paper outlines improved methods for the investigation of cases.

356. Stevenson, I. (1961-62). **Comments on Parapsychology and "reincarnation" by Professor C. T. K. Chari.** Indian Journal of Parapsychology, 3, 22-26.

Stevenson counters some of Chari's critical comments regarding reincarnation. He defends the plausibility of the reincarnation hypothesis. (See Chari, 1961-62.)

357. Stevenson, I. (1961-62). **Introduction to "A case suggestive of reincarnation in West Bengal" by Professor P. Pal.** Indian Journal of Parapsychology, 3, 1-4.

Support is added to the reincarnation theory as an explanation of the case presented. (See also Pal, 1961-62.)

358. Stevenson, I. (1961). **Methods of investigating some alleged cases of reincarnation in India.** Journal of Parapsychology, 25, 287-288.

This is a brief abstract from the Fourth Annual PA Convention where a panel discussion on postmortem survival was held. Stevenson summarizes the method of investigating children's alleged reports of reincarnation.

359. Stevenson, I. (1966). **Cultural patterns in cases suggestive of reincarnation among the Tlingit Indians of southeastern Alaska.** Journal of the American Society for Psychical Research, 60, 229-243.

Cultural factors appear to influence the features and incidence of cases suggestive of reincarnation. The frequency of blood relationships, birth marks, and "announcing" dreams characterize the reports. Certain aspects of the Tlingit culture emphasize these features, which in turn influence the culture. Out of 29 "announcing" dreams, 26 correctly predicted the sex of the "reborn" (expected baby).

360. Stevenson, I. (1970). **Characteristics of cases of the reincarnation type in Turkey and their comparison with cases in two other cultures.** International Journal of Comparative Sociology, 11, 1-17.

Reincarnation cases among the Turkish Alevis are compared with cases from the Sinhalese and Tamil in Ceylon (Sri Lanka) and the Tlingit Indians of Alaska. Similarities include the typically young age of the subjects, but the cases differ in the proportion of cases in which both subject and previous person belonged to the same family, the mode of death of the previous person, the incidence and character of birthmarks and announcing dreams, as well as in the proportion of cases in which the previous person is identified. Almost all of the Alevis and Tlingit cases are verified, but only half of the Ceylonese are.

361. Stevenson, I. (1971). **The belief in reincarnation and related cases among the Eskimos of Alaska** [Summary]. In W. G. Roll, R. L. Morris, & J. D. Morris (Eds.), Proceedings of the Parapsychological Association 1969, 6 (pp. 53-55). Durham, NC: Parapsychological Association.

Fifteen cases of Eskimo children who claim to remember previous lives are compared to a larger number of similar cases from among the neighboring Tlingit Indians.

362. Stevenson, I. (1972). **Some new cases suggestive of reincarnation. I. The case of Rajul Shah.** Journal of the American Society for Psychical Research, 66, 288-309.

From the age of 2 1/2 years, Rajul Shah spoke of past life memories. At age nine, these claims were investigated. The past life memories focused mainly on the features of the house, members of the family (who were accurately identified in person), food, play, and religious worship.

363. Stevenson, I. (1972). **Some new cases suggestive of reincarnation. II. The case of Bishen Chand.** Journal of the American Society for Psychical Research, 66, 375-400.

A fully investigated account of Bishen Chand, who at age three gave detailed accounts of his past life.

364. Stevenson, I. (1973). **Some new cases suggestive of reincarnation. III. The case of Suleyman Andary.** Journal of the American Society for Psychical Research, 67, 244-266.

At five or six years of age, Suleyman Andary had recollections of a past life. At 11 years of age, more details were recounted. Stevenson goes into Andary's background and explores the memories presented. An explanation of possible reincarnation is given.

365. Stevenson, I. (1973). **Some new cases suggestive of reincarnation. IV. The case of Ampan Petcherat.** Journal of the American Society for Psychical Research, 67, 361-380.

This is the case of a girl who claimed to remember from age one details in a life as a boy. The article also discusses "sex change" reincarnation across cultures, noting that some cultures report none, while others report up to 20%.

366. Stevenson, I. (1973). **Carington's psychon theory as applied to cases of the reincarnation type: A reply to Gardner Murphy.** Journal of the American Society for Psychical Research, 67, 130-145.

A reply to Murphy (see Murphy, 1973) who proposed Carington's association theory of mind as an explanation of children's past life memories. Although some features of such cases fit the assumptions of Carington's theory, many others do not. Of particular importance are the emotions displayed by many of the children in reporting their memories.

367. Stevenson, I. (1973). **Characteristics of case of the reincarnation type in Ceylon.** Contributions to Asian Studies, 3, 26-29.

This presents a summary analysis of 40 cases of children who claim to remember previous lives in Ceylon (now Sri Lanka). In an unusually high proportion of cases (in 23 of the 40 cases) the previous person was not identified.

368. Stevenson, I. (1973). **The "perfect" reincarnation case** [Summary]. In W. G. Roll, R. L. Morris, & J. D. Morris (Eds.), Research in Parapsychology 1972 (pp. 185-187). Metuchen, NJ: Scarecrow Press.

This describes a hypothetical "perfect" reincarnation case, in which a French child had veridical memories of a man who lived and died in Ceylon (Sri Lanka), had birthmarks which resembled that person's death wounds, and who behaved in ways characteristic of that person. These features, which appear separately in many cases, if combined in one case would present a strong challenge to the ESP explanation of past life memory cases.

369. Stevenson, I. (1974). **Some new cases suggestive of reincarnation. V. The case of Indika Guneratne.** Journal of the American Society for Psychical Research, 68, 58-90.

From age three to four and one-half years, Indika spoke of a past life in which he had been wealthy, enjoyed gambling, and owned an estate. The child often commented that in his present life, his house was too small, his clothes were shabby, and his food was meager. The case was investigated when he was six years of age.

370. Stevenson, I. (1974). **Some questions related to cases of the reincarnation type.** Journal of the American Society for Psychical Research, 68, 395-416.

This offers tentative answers to eight questions frequently asked about reincarnation. The questions concern: the relationship between reincarnation cases and culture, the collective unconscious as an explanation for the cases, whether all persons reincarnate or some only, karma, what reincarnates, why all persons might not recall previous lives, hypnosis as an aid to memory, and memories of experiences between death and rebirth.

371. Stevenson, I. (1974). **Two cases of the reincarnation type with written records made before verifications** [Summary]. In W. G. Roll, R. L. Morris, & J. D. Morris (Eds.), Research in Parapsychology 1973 (pp. 60-63). Metuchen, NJ: Scarecrow Press.

This describes two cases from Ceylon (Sri Lanka) of children who claimed to have memories of previous lives. In the first of these cases the author made a written record of the child's statements before he verified them. In the second case, the written record was made and verified by a monk who was a relative of the family, but the author subsequently made his own investigation. More detailed reports of both cases are contained in volume III of the author's series, Cases of the Reincarnation Type, Stevenson, I., 1980.

372. Stevenson, I. (1975). **The belief and cases related to reincarnation among the Haida.** Journal of Anthropological Research, 31, 364-375.

This describes characteristics of 24 cases of children who claim to remember previous lives among the Haida, an Indian tribe in Alaska and British Columbia, and compares them with similar cases from other cultures. Haida cases resemble cases of other Indian tribes in northwestern North America, but they differ in some ways from cases in other parts of the world.

373. Stevenson, I. (1977). **The explanatory value of the idea of reincarnation.** Journal of Nervous and Mental Disease, 164, 305-326.

This is a thorough overview of investigations, distributions, and analyses conducted on reincarnation cases. There is discussion of the contribution of reincarnation to the understanding of phobias and philias of childhood, abnormalities of child-parent relationships, skills not learned in early life, vendettas, childhood sexuality and gender identity confusions, birth marks, congenital deformities, etc. Ample supportive case histories are included.

374. Stevenson, I. (1977). **Research into the evidence of man's survival after death: A historical and critical survey with a summary of recent developments.** Journal of Nervous and Mental Disease, 165, 152-170.

This is a critical, in-depth survey covering evidence and research on survival from ancient civilizations to the present. Three pages are devoted to reincarnation cases in which children, usually between two and four years, seem to remember past lives. Included are difficulties encountered in past research and over seventy references.

375. Stevenson, I. (1977). **The belief in reincarnation and cases of the reincarnation type among the Haida.** Journal of the American Society for Psychical Research, 71, 177-189.

This is a slightly revised version of the author's study of Haida Indian reincarnation cases published in the Journal of Anthropological Research, Stevenson, I., 1975.

376. Stevenson, I. (1979). **What next in survival research?: 6. The search for the less than perfect case of the reincarnation type.** Journal of Indian Psychology 2, 30-34.

Paramnesia (faulty memory) is emerging as the strongest interpretation of past life memory cases as the alternative to reincarnation. The problem of paramnesia can most successfully be overcome in cases where written records are made of a subject's statements before their verification. Seven Indian cases of this type are on file, representing half of the worldwide total. India would, therefore, seem a promising place to obtain other cases, but more workers are needed.

377. Stevenson, I. (1983). **American children who claim to remember previous lives.** Journal of Nervous and Mental Disease, 171, 742-748.

Cases of 79 American children (43 male and 36 female, age at time of interview not given) claiming to remember past lives are analyzed and compared to 266 similar cases in India. American children began speaking about the apparent memories earlier (mean age 37 months) than Indian children (mean age 38 months) and stopped speaking about them sooner (mean age 64 months) than Indian children (mean age 79 months). American children speak of deceased friends or relatives of their family, as compared to India, where memories are of another family that is often in another community. There are few verifiable statements of American children due to fewer specific statements of names. Similarities of cases in both cultures include age of child's first speaking about the previous life, high incidence of violent death in previous life, and unusual behavior on the part of the child, corresponding to the statement about apparent memories.

378. Stevenson, I. (1986). **Characteristics of cases of the reincarnation type among the Igbo of Nigeria.** Journal of Asian and African Studies, 21, 204-216.

Cases of Igbo children who claim to remember previous lives are compared to cases from nine other cultures on a series of variables. Although the cases of all cultures are similar in form overall, there are differences from one to another in features such as the proportion of cases with changes of sex between lives, the proportion of cases with violent death, and the length of the interval between lives.

379. Stevenson, I. (1990). **Phobias in children who claim to remember previous lives.** Journal of Scientific Exploration, 4, 243-254.

Of 387 cases of children who claimed to remember previous lives in which the previous personality was identified, 141 (36%) included pronounced phobias. Most often the phobias corresponded to the death the previous personality suffered. The phobias usually appeared when the child was between 2 and 5 and sometimes manifested before the child began to speak about the previous life. The phobias could not be explained as imitations of another member of the family or as results of a postnatal traumatic experience. The author discusses possible explanations for the phobias, among them reincarnation.

380. Stevenson, I. & Chadha, N. (1990). **Can children be stopped from speaking about previous lives? Some further analyses of features of cases of the reincarnation type.** Journal of the Society for Psychical Research, 56, 82-90.

This reports additional analyses made by the authors of cases of Indian children who speak about previous lives. In 29 (41%) of 69 cases families tried to suppress the children's memories, but these efforts were not successful. Although children whose memories were suppressed stopped speaking about the lives they remembered at a slightly younger age than children whose memories were not suppressed, the difference was not statistically significant.

381. Stevenson. I. & Edelstein, S. J. (1982). **The belief in reincarnation among the Igbo of southeastern Nigeria, with particular reference to connections between the ogbanje ("repeater babies") and sickle cell anemia** [Summary]. In W. G. Roll, R. L. Morris, & R. A. White (Eds.), Research in Parapsychology 1981 (pp. 178-179). Metuchen, NJ: Scarecrow Press.

The Igbo believe everyone reincarnates, and children who die young may be reborn in the same family to die young again. The Ogbanje die young in order to harass their parents. Ritualistic acts to prevent repeated death are discussed.

382. Stevenson, I., Pasricha, S., & Samararatne, G. (1988). **Deception and self-deception in cases of reincarnation type: Seven illustrative cases in Asia.** Journal of the American Society for Psychical Research, 82, 1-31.

Seven supposed reincarnation cases in Asia, which were initially thought to be authentic, were found to be fraudulent after interviews with the informants. The authors stress that judgment about authenticity requires independent verification of a subject's statements.

383. Stevenson, I., Prasad, J., Mehrotra, L. P., & Rawat, K. S. (1974). **The investigation of cases of the reincarnation type in India.** Contributions to Asian Studies, 5, 36-49.

This describes an ongoing research program to locate and investigate cases of claimed past life memory in India. The majority of cases on file involve Hindu children in northern India. Possible ways of understanding the cases are considered, with reincarnation found to be the most defensible.

384. Stevenson, I. & Samararatne, G. (1988). **Three new cases of the reincarnation type in Sri Lanka with written records made before verifications.** Journal of Scientific Exploration, 2, 217-238.

This describes cases of three children in Sri Lanka who claimed to remember previous lives. Two of the children were about 3 years and the third was between 3 and 4 when they first began to speak of their memories. In all three cases, written records of the children's statements were made by the authors before they were verified. In two of these cases, over 80% of the recorded statements were found to be correct, and in the third case, over 90% were correct.

385. Stevenson, I. & Story, F. (1970). **A case of the reincarnation type in Ceylon: The case of Disna Samarasinghe.** Journal of Asian and African Studies, 5, 241-255.

When she was 3 years old, Disna Samarasinghe, watching her mother wash clothes, suddenly told her that she had washed clothes herself at her home in another town. It emerged that she was talking about herself in a previous life. Over the next several months, Disna made other statements about the life of the woman she said she had been, and showed a precocious aptitude for various household chores. Her memories were detailed enough that the woman she was talking about was identified. (A fuller report of this case is contained in the second volume of Stevenson's Cases of the reincarnation type; see under **Books and Articles**, Stevenson, 1977.)

386. Stevenson, I., Williams, E. F., Pasricha, S., Samararatne, G., & Maung, U W. (1981). **The problem of "unsolved" cases of the reincarnation type** [Summary]. In W. G. Roll & J. Beloff (Eds.), Research in Parapsychology 1980 (pp. 111-113). Metuchen, NJ: Scarecrow Press.

A study of unsolved cases yielded several factors that contributed to the failure to solve a case: 1) the subject had not given enough specific information; 2) names were mispronounced or misremembered; 3) faulty inferences misled; 4) real previous life memories were mixed with current life memories and fantasies; 5) there was a lack of interest in solving the case; 6) others suppressed verifying information; 7) the case was not pursued enough.

387. Story, F. & Stevenson, I. (1967). **A case of the reincarnation type in Ceylon: The case of Warnasiri Adikari.** Journal of the American Society for Psychical Research, 61, 130-145.

This describes investigation of a four-year-old boy, who recounted a previous life in a village some six miles from his home. Precognitive experiences, related to his "past life" family who were alive at the time, are noted. Recall of three previous lives before this one is also included. The authors conclude that the child had paranormally derived information about the previous personality.

Books and Articles

388. Almeder, R. (1987). Beyond death: Evidence for life after death Springfield, IL: Thomas.

This contains a long chapter reviewing Stevenson's research with children who claim to remember previous lives. The author is strongly supportive of Stevenson's work.

389. Chari, C. T. K. (1962). **How good is the evidence for reincarnation?** Tomorrow, 89-98.

Chari discusses several well-known reincarnation cases and finds the evidence for paranormality wanting.

390. Chari, C. T. K. (1978). **Reincarnation research: Method and interpretation.** In M. Ebon (Ed.), Signet handbook of parapsychology, (pp. 313-324). NY: NAL Books.

This is a critical appraisal of research on children's past life memories. Two inauthentic cases are briefly described.

391. Cook, E. W. (1986). **Research on reincarnation type cases: Present status and suggestions for future research.** In K. R. Rao (Ed.), Case studies in parapsychology (pp. 87-96). Jefferson, NC: McFarland.

This provides an overview of the research program at the University of Virginia. Efforts at improving the reincarnation database are aimed at finding more cases early in their development, more cases with birthmarks and birth defects, and more cases involving twins. Cook also describes difficulties she encountered while investigating cases in Lebanon.

392. Durant, R. (Ed.). (1968). Totality man. London: Regency Press.

This contains investigative reports of children with past life memories from India, Ceylon (Sri Lanka), Burma, and Turkey.

393. Edelstein, S. J. (1986). The sickled cell: From myths to molecules Cambridge, MA: Harvard University Press.

This book is a general introduction to research on sickled cell anemia. Much of it is technical, but it includes a lengthy discussion of the author's investigation (with I. Stevenson) of children identified as the latest incarnations of children who are believed to have been born and died prematurely several times before in the same family. Some scientists have suggested that the "repeater child" concept reflects the native understanding of sickled cell anemia, but blood tests conducted by Edelstein and Stevenson ruled out this possibility.

394. Gauld, A. (1982). Mediumship and survival: A century of investigations. London: Heinemann.

Gauld appraises the evidence for reincarnation, including that of Stevenson's research on children's past life memories. He is inclined to agree with Stevenson's interpretation of the cases as suggestive of reincarnation.

395. Hind, C. (1977). **The reincarnation of Vashnee Rattan.** Fate, Jan., 58-64.

A four-year-old South African girl began to relate memories of a previous life after accompanying her father on a business trip. She said she had been a child who had died of dysentery at 9 years of age 20 years before, and recognized people and places connected with the life of this child; her memories were verified.

396. Klausner, M. (1975). Reincarnation. Ramat-Gan, Israel: Massada.

This includes several cases of Israeli Druse children who claim to remember previous lives. Some of the cases are verified. The author is head of the Israeli Society for Parapsychology.

397. Lenz, F. (1979). Lifetimes: true accounts of reincarnation. Indianapolis: Bobbs Merrill.

Although basically about the past life visions of adults, this book includes one account of an American child who recalled a previous life as a Navy officer killed at Pearl Harbor (pp. 172-175).

398. Matlock, J. G. (1988). **The decline of past life memory with the subject's age in spontaneous reincarnation cases.** In M. L. Albertson, D. S. Ward, & K. P. Freeman (Eds.), Paranormal research (pp. 388-401). Fort Collins, CO: Rocky Mountain Research Institute.

This describes a series of cases previously reported by I. Stevenson that reveal how past life memories change in strength the older the subject is when first having the memories. The younger the child, the stronger and better developed the memories are.

399. Matlock, J. G. (1990). **Past life memory case studies.** In S. Krippner (Ed.), Advances in parapsychological research 6 (pp. 184-267). Jefferson, NC: McFarland.

This is a comprehensive review of research on past life memory cases, covering spontaneous past life memory cases (most of which involve young children), statistical studies of cases, and commentary on the research. The author concludes that the evidence, taken as a whole, seems better interpreted in terms of reincarnation than in terms of culturally conditioned fantasy, but that a final judgment in favor of reincarnation must wait until the evidence can be assimilated to the rest of scientific knowledge.

400. Merle, S. A. (1976). **A case of reincarnation in America: Four year old Natalie remembers.** Fate, June, 53-56.

This is a mother's description of the apparent past life memories of her adopted daughter. The apparent memories include details of events that occurred after death in that life, but are unverified.

401. Prasad, J. (1973). **Parapsychology in India.** In A. Angoff & B. Shapin (Eds.), Parapsychology today: A geographical view (pp. 43-52). NY: Parapsychology Foundation.

This contains a description of a questionnaire study which compared the personalities of the subjects and previous persons in six verified past life memory cases. Strong similarities were found in four of the six cases (pp. 46-47).

402. Rawat, K. S. (1985). **A case suggestive of reincarnation.** Venture Inward, 1(8), 10-12.

This describes the case of a child who, at two-and-a-half years of age, began to speak about a previous life. Later, he recognized a woman he saw as his mother of that life, and she verified what he had been saying. Features of the case are typical of features of over 100 cases collected by the author's Institute for Research in Parapsychology in Beawar, India.

403. Rogo, D. S. (1985). The search for yesterday: A critical examination of the evidence for reincarnation. Englewood Cliffs, NJ: Prentice Hall.

This is a critical review of evidence for reincarnation, including cases of children who remember previous lives.

Reviewed by: Anderson, R. I. (1987). Journal of the American Society for Psychical Research, 81, 193-196. Matlock, J. G., with Comments by I. Stevenson (1986). Journal of the Society for Psychical Research, 53, 229-238.

404. Shirley, R. (1936). The Problem of Rebirth: The basis of the reincarnationistic hypothesis. London: Rider.

This is a collection of cases and discussions relating to reincarnation. Many of the cases, summarized or reprinted from other books, newspapers, or periodicals, involve young children.

405. Stevenson, I. (1966). Twenty cases suggestive of reincarnation. NY: American Society for Psychical Research.

This reviews in detail twenty cases of children recounting memories of former lives. The author offers various hypotheses, but concludes that reincarnation appears a viable possibility.

Reviewed by: Rhine, L. E. (1966). Journal of Parapsychology, 30, 263-272. Reply: Stevenson, I. (1967), Journal of Parapsychology, 31, 149-154.

406. Stevenson, I. (1974). Twenty cases suggestive of reincarnation, 2nd ed. Charlottesville: University Press of Virginia.

This is a revised edition of the author's classic study, originally published in the Proceedings of the American Society for Psychical Research. It includes the results of follow-up interviews with 17 of the 20 child subjects.

Reviewed by: Beloff, J. (1975). Journal of the Society for Psychical Research, 48, 177-179.

407. Stevenson, I. (1974). **Xenoglossy: A review and report of a case.** Proceedings of the American Society for Psychical Research, 31, 1-268. (Reprinted in 1974 by University Press of Virginia, Charlottesville.)

Xenoglossy is the purported ability to use correctly a language unlearned in the present life. Several examples of children who have employed xenoglossy in past life memory cases are reviewed (pp. 14-18).

408. Stevenson, I. (1975). Cases of the reincarnation type. Vol. I. Ten cases from India. Charlottesville: University Press of Virginia.

This includes reports of children with past life memories selected from hundreds of Indian cases. The book reviews problems in investigating and validating reincarnation cases in general and specific problems encountered in working in India. Each case is reviewed in detail with names, dates, and familial reactions.

Reviewed by: Beloff, J. (1976). Journal of the Society for Psychical Research, 48, 306-309.

409. Stevenson, I. (1977). Cases of the reincarnation type. Vol. II. Ten cases in Sri Lanka. Charlottesville: University Press of Virginia.

This is the second volume in a series on children's past life memories. Cases abstracted are from those gathered in Sri Lanka. The book includes an introductory chapter describing the belief in reincarnation in Sri Lanka.

Reviewed by: Brody, E. R. (1979). Journal of the American Society for Psychical Research, 73, 71-81.

410. Stevenson, I. (1977). **Reincarnation: Field studies and theoretical issues.** In B. B. Wolman (Ed.), Handbook of parapsychology (pp. 631-663). NY: Van Nostrand Reinhold.

This is an overview of research with children who say they remember previous lives. A detailed report of a Lebanese Druse case is included.

411. Stevenson, I. (1980). Cases of the reincarnation type. Vol. III. Twelve cases in Lebanon and Turkey. Charlottesville: University Press of Virginia.

This is the third volume in a series on children's past life memories, presenting detailed reports of cases among the Druse of Lebanon and the Alevis of Turkey. The book includes discussions of Druse and Alevi reincarnation beliefs and concludes with a general discussion of the author's reincarnation studies.

Reviewed by: Owen, A. R. G. (1981). Journal of the American Society for Psychical Research, 75, 345-348.

412. Stevenson, I. (1983). Cases of the reincarnation type. Vol. IV. Twelve cases in Thailand and Burma. Charlottesville: University Press of Virginia.

This is the fourth volume in the author's series of detailed reincarnation case reports. Most of the cases involve young children.

Reviewed by: Chari, C. T. K. (1986). Journal of the Society for Psychical Research, 53, 325-329. Gauld, A. (1985). Journal of the American Society for Psychical Research, 79, 80-85.

413. Stevenson, I. (1987). Children who remember previous lives: A question of reincarnation. Charlottesville: University Press of Virginia.

This is a summary of the author's study, over 30 years, of children who say they remember previous lives. The book includes summaries of six cases not previously reported in detail, including some from the United States. Other chapters cover methods of research, the explanatory value of the idea of reincarnation, and speculations about processes possibly related to reincarnation.

Reviewed by: Almeder, R. (1990). Journal of the American Society for Psychical Research, 84, 88-93. Hess, D. J. (1988). Parapsychology Review, 19(4), 8-10. Wilson, I. (1988). Journal of the Society for Psychical Research, 55, 227-229. The Wilson review is followed by a response from Stevenson (pp. 230-234).

414. Story, F. (1975). Rebirth as doctrine and experience: Essays and case studies. (Collected works, vol. 2). Kandy, Sri Lanka: Buddhist Publishing Society.

The reincarnation cases described in this volume occurred in Ceylon (Sri Lanka) and Burma. They were investigated by Story, sometimes in association with Ian Stevenson. The book includes a chapter on children's claimed memories of the period between death and rebirth.

415. Wambach, H. (1978). Reliving past lives: The evidence of over one thousand past life recalls. NY: Barnes and Noble.

This book is mainly about regressions to previous lives under hypnosis, but it includes the account of an American child who claimed to remember the life of a policeman and began to act out his memories (pp. 5-6).

416. Wilson, I. (1982). All in the mind: Reincarnation, hypnotic regression, stigmata, multiple personality, and other little understood powers of the mind. Garden City, NY: Doubleday.

Wilson reports on his investigations into the case of the English Pollock twins, who as young children seemed to remember the lives of their dead sisters. Two chapters are devoted to a critical review of Ian Stevenson's research.

VII. MISCELLANEOUS

VII. MISCELLANEOUS

417. Barrett, W. F. (1886-87). **On some physical phenomena commonly called spiritualistic, witnessed by the author.** Proceedings of the Society for Psychical Research, 4, 25-42.

This recounts two cases of spiritualistic-like phenomena. One involves a young girl, age 10, where raps, sounds of moving furniture and sounds of nails being hammered occurred with the child and author alone in a room. The child was in various positions around the room to help rule out fraud. Events ceased three months later. A second case was reported of a middle-aged woman, with similar phenomena occurring. The author offers possibilities for future research and discussion about these cases.

418. Bush, N. (1983). **The near-death experience in children: Shades of the prison-house reopening.** Anabiosis, 3, 177-193.

Retrospective accounts of near-death experiences by 17 children (ages 13 months to 14 years) showed that NDEs in childhood are similar in content to those experienced by adults. Noted are commonalities such as a light or dark tunnel, sense of well-being, out-of-body experience, and absence of fear.

419. Crookall, R. (1963). **An infant's perception of a death.** Journal of the Society for Psychical Research, 42, 124-126.

A two year old recounts seeing an apparition of a grandfather who had died suddenly. Confirmatory statements from the family are included.

420. Dallas, H. A. (1935). **Concerning the death of infants.** Quarterly Transactions of the British College of Psychic Science, 14, 160-164.

This reviews experiences collected in the book The Nurseries of Heaven, by H. A. Dallas and G. V. Owen. It gives descriptions of infants who die and are seen in their spirit form near their parents, and it gives a case example.

421. Gower, J. H. (1913-14). **Musical prodigies and automatism.** Journal of the Society for Psychical Research, 16, 56-64.

Two musical prodigies, a 3 1/2-year-old boy and a 10-year-old girl, who play the piano without ever having had instruction, are discussed. The question of reincarnation is explored.

422. Greyson, B. (1986). **Incidence of near-death experiences following attempted suicide.** Suicide and Life Threatening Behavior, 16, 40-45.

Among 61 hospitalized patients who had attempted suicide, 16 (ages 17-62) reported NDEs precipitated by the attempt. Subjects had significantly higher scores on the mystical consciousness, depersonalization, and hyperalterness factors using the Weighted Core Experience Index.

423. Herzog, D. B. & Herrin, J. T. (1985). **Near-death experiences in the very young.** Critical Care Medicine, 13, 1074-1075.

This reports the case of a six-month old child who was admitted to an intensive care unit with a severe illness. She recovered, but from then on she panicked whenever she was encouraged to crawl through a play tunnel at a local department store. When she was three and a half, upon hearing that her grandmother was near death, she asked, "Will Grandma have to go through the tunnel at the store to get to God?" The tunnel image is a common feature of near-death experiences with children and adults.

424. Hope, O. (1941-42). **Greek script by a child of four.** Journal of the Society for Psychical Research, 32, 116-119.

The case of a four-year-old girl who was able to write Greek letters is explored. The child's father felt that the words might be a message from his father, a Greek scholar, who had been in the habit of communicating in Greek to him. The child never wrote any other letters previously, either in English or any other language.

425. Lambert, G. (1966). **An apparition of a child: The case of Johnnie M.** Journal of the Society for Psychical Research, 43, 428-431.

A woman, sleeping in the room where a child had died, sees an apparition.

426. Lang, A. (1895). **The voices of Jeanne D'Arc.** Proceedings of the Society for Psychical Research, 11, 198-212.

This recounts various phenomena exhibited by Joan of Arc from the age of thirteen.

427. Leaning, F. E. (1928). **Calculating boy.** British Journal of Psychical Research, 1, 374-381.

A blind boy (age 15) who was very slow mentally, was able to do elaborate and complex mental math calculations. Other cases of a similar kind are cited and discussed from a psychic phenomena perspective.

428. Levinson, L. E. (1968). **Hypnosis: the key to unlocking latent psi faculties.** International Journal of Parapsychology, 10, 117-147.

The hypothesis that "hypnosis is a catalyst for unlocking psi faculties" is investigated. Four males and one female (ages 16-35) are tested over a nine-year period. Results indicate that factors in the augmentation of psi faculties are: 1) the degree of rapport between hypnotist and subject; 2) the working hypnosis technique; and 3) the achievement of deep trance.

429. Lodge, O. (1909-10) **Possible automatism of young children.** Journal of the Society for Psychical Research, 14, 60-62.

The cases of young musical prodigies who are able to play the piano by instinct, long before they could have learned to play and/or write music, are discussed. The author offers possible explanations for the phenomena and ways for parents to handle their reactions.

430. Montgomery, E. E. (1940). **An account of some extraordinary psychic experiences with Alice Belle Kirby.** Journal of the American Society for Psychical Research, 34, 275-284.

A fourteen-year-old girl, living in Jonesville, Louisiana, has been demonstrating various mediumship feats, such as physical levitation, for two and one-half years. The article is written by a family friend.

431. Moody, R. A. (1988). **The light beyond.** New Age Journal, 5, 55-67.

Near-death experiences are discussed in terms of patterns similar to all ages, and counter-arguments are given to various theories about NDEs. Follow-up studies are reviewed, particularly as to the impact the NDE had on the person's spiritual beliefs and emotional well-being. Children (ages 3-16) who have experienced NDEs were interviewed and found to have similar experiences to adults, in marked contrast to non-NDE children.

432. Morse, M. (1983). **A near-death experience in a 7-year-old child.** American Journal of Diseases of Children, 137, 959-961.

This reports the near-death experience of a 7-year-old girl who nearly drowned in a swimming pool. Her Mormon religious background colored her interpretation of the experience, but the structure of the experience was similar to other near-death experiences.

433. Morse, M., Catillo, P., Venecia, D., Milstein, J., & Tyler, D. C.(1986). **Childhood near-death experiences.** American Journal of Diseases of Children, 140, 1110-1114.

Interviews were conducted with 11 children, ages 3 through 13 years, who had survived critical illnesses. Near-death experiences were reported by seven of them. Another 27 hospitalized children were interviewed, but none of these reported memories while they were supposed to have been unconscious. A neurophysiological explanation of the NDE is presented.

434. Neppe, V. M. (1984). **Subjective paranormal experience psychosis.** Parapsychology Review, 15, 7-9.

Four cases experiencing "psychic psychosis" are reported. Each had a large number of subjective paranormal experiences in childhood, and three had sudden forebodings of their own death which were associated with their decompensation. Precognitive, telepathic, and psychokinetic experiences were reported. One of the cases was an 18-year-old boy.

435. Nicol, F. (1979). **Fraudulent children in psychical research.** Parapsychology Review, 10, 16-21.

The article gives a historical overview of deceit and mischief used by children and teenagers in renowned cases of mediumship, psychokinesis, telepathy, and mini-Gellers. The author suggests that researchers can easily misinterpret events where fraud is intended.

436. Pasricha, S. & Stevenson, I. (1986). **Near-death experiences in India.** Journal of Nervous and Mental Disease, 174, 165-170.

This article features 16 cases of adult near-death experiences investigated in India. All cases are from events occurring at a median age of 35 years, with the first investigation occurring approximately 14 years after the event. One case was of a 54-year-old man recounting an NDE occurring at age 10. In these cases, Indian and American NDEs resemble each other in some respects, but differ in that in Indian NDEs, percipients do not see their own physical body during the NDE.

437. Prasad, J. & Stevenson, I. A. (1968). **A survey of spontaneous psychical experiences in school children of Uttar Pradesh, India.** International Journal of Parapsychology, 10, 241-261.

Zener cards were administered to 2,500 8th graders (ages 11-13) following a talk on the objectives of the experiment and the completion of a questionnaire by the students. Results showed that 36% of the students had psi experiences, with the majority being contemporary rather than precognitive in nature. Psi dreams were found to be the most frequent type of experience. Also included is a discussion of: 1) commonality of spontaneous psi experiences, 2) Indian cultural factors affecting types of psi phenomena reported, and 3) types of phenomena related to the students' ages.

438. Rhine, J. B. (1948). **Conditions favoring success in psi tests.** Journal of Parapsychology, 12, 58-75.

This describes tests conducted with children and how the interest of the subject is an important factor when creating an experiment. It discusses types of experiments that work well with children (pp. 63-69).

439. Rhine, J. B. (1964). **Special motivation in some exceptional ESP performances.** Journal of Parapsychology, 28, 42-50.

Examples of extraordinarily high scoring produced by seven different subjects over the last 30 years are studied in relation to special motivation. Two nine-year-old girls, one seven-year-old girl, and one ten-year-old boy comprise the sample.

440. Richet, C. (1901). **A musical prodigy.** Journal of the Society for Psychical Research, 10, 20-22.

This records the case of a 3 1/2-year-old Spanish boy who could play the piano and write music. He was able to play 20 pieces of music by memory without instruction or practice. No explanation for this ability was offered.

441. Roney-Dougal, S. M. (1989). **Recent findings relating to the possible role of the pineal gland in affecting psychic ability.** Journal of the Society for Psychical Research, 55, 313-328.

In an article on the role of the pineal gland in affecting psi ability, the author mentions that children have higher concentrations of melatonin and beta-carbolenes than do adults. The author links the presence of beta-carbolenes to instances of psi.

442. Serdahely, W. J. (1989-90). **A pediatric near-death experience: Tunnel variants.** Omega, 20, 55-62.

An 8-year-old boy reported a near-death experience after nearly drowning. While in the "tunnel," rather than seeing deceased friends or relatives, he saw two of his family's pets that had previously died. Tunnel experiences involved in both child and adult NDE's are discussed.

443. Solfvin, G., Roll, W. G., & Krieger, J. (1978). **Meditation and ESP: Remote viewing** [Summary]. In W.G. Roll (Ed.), Research in Parapsychology 1977 (pp. 151-157). Metuchen, NJ: Scarecrow Press.

Sixteen high school students (ages 16-19) were instructed in ENO meditation. One student was randomly selected to act as agent in a remote viewing task. The group then meditated on the target location. Results indicated no significant psi scoring via majority vote or through individual performances.

444. Thomas, L. E., Cooper, P. E., & Suscovich, D. J. (1983). **Incidence of near-death and intense spiritual experiences in an intergenerational sample: An Interpretation.** Omega, 13, 35-41.

Results were analyzed from a structural and open-ended questionnaire survey of 305 people (ages 17-85). A total of 120 young adults (ages 17-29) were included in the sample. Of this age group, 26% reported near-death experiences, while 33% reported intense spiritual experiences. The middle-aged group (ages 30-59) reported the highest percentage in both categories. Sixty percent of the total sample who reported a near-death experience were significantly ($p < .001$) more likely to report an intense spiritual experience as well.

445. Tobacyk, J., Miller, M. L., & Jones, G. (1984). **Paranormal beliefs of high school students.** Psychological Reports, 55, 253-261.

The Paranormal Belief Scale was administered to 95 boys and 98 girls in the 11th grade. Results were compared with those from a sample of 424 college students. High school students showed significantly less belief than college students on the total Paranormal Scale and on the subscales of Psi belief, Extraordinary Life Forms, and Witchcraft, and were greater disbelievers in paranormal phenomena. The number of science courses taken correlated significantly ($p < .05$) and inversely with total Paranormal Scale scores, Traditional Religious Belief scores, and Psi Belief scores. Traditional Religious Belief scores were significantly directly associated with the grade point average ($p = .21$).

446. Twemlow, S. W. & Gabbard, G. (1984-5). **The influence of demographic/psychological factors and pre-existing conditions on the near-death experience.** Omega, 15, 223-235.

Out of a larger survey of 386 respondents having out-of-body experiences, 34 participants (ages 12-76) reported near-death states (at 3.5 to 60 years). They were examined for pre-existing conditions, demographic, psychological, physical, and perceptual-cognitive differences. Evidence was seen of a different perceptual-cognitive style in NDEs, including a tendency to be significantly more attention-absorbed.

447. Twemlow, S. W., Gabbard, G. O., & Jones, F. C. (1982). **The out-of-body experience: A phenomenological typology based on questionnaire responses.** American Journal of Psychiatry, 139, 450-455.

A survey of 339 respondents who had OBEs (ages 12-83, with a mean age of 44.4 years) were compared to 81 who had not. A significantly greater proportion of the respondents experiencing OBEs when mentally calm were meditators ($p <$ .0001). Results did not support that drugs, religious conditioning, pre-existing psychopathology, or esoteric belief systems influence OBEs. Phenomenological characteristics were similar to those reported by other researchers. This survey does not break down the respondents by age groups or frequency, and many of the experiences were reported as having occurred years before.

448. White, R. A. (1987). Parapsychology for Parents: A bibliographic guide. Dix Hills, NY: Parapsychology Sources of Information Center. [Unannotated.]

The bibliography includes sections on: Information about parapsychology, Testing ESP and PK, Children and parapsychology, Sources on the parent-child relationship and psi, Sources aimed at parents, Books on parapsychology written for young people, Glossary of parapsychological and related terms, Addresses of parapsychological organizations cited.

Books and Articles

449. Alter, S. (1979). **Mother and child: The ESP bond.** Parents, 54(9), 34-38.

A general article reviews aspects of mother-child telepathy, clairvoyance, the emotional link facilitating psi phenomena, and testing your child. Several noted parapsychology researchers are quoted.

450. Burns, L. (1988). Develop your child's psychic abilities. NY: Pocket Books.

This is a practical how-to book of psychic development geared for parents. The book offers information on identifying whether your child is psychic, understanding the psychic child's needs, and discussing invisible friends. There are exercises for encouraging expression and awareness of psychic abilities through psychic readings, psychometry, reading auras, psychic healing, clairvoyance, PK, levitation, mediumship, and telepathy.

451. Cooke, A. H. (1968). Out of the mouths of babes. Cambridge: James Clarke & Co.

This is an anecdotal collection of psychic experiences exhibited by children. The material covers astral projection, precognition, reincarnation, children's death-bed experiences, and miscellaneous cases.

452. Drucker, S. A. & Drewes, A. A. (1977). **Children and ESP.** American Society for Psychical Research Newsletter, 3(3), 1-2.

This is an article describing ways to test children for ESP, types of tests to use, factors affecting their performance, and how to handle a child's psychic abilities.

453. Gabbard, G. O. & Twemlow, S. W. (1984). With the eyes of the mind: An Empirical Analysis of Out-of-Body States. NY: Praeger.

Although this book is about the out-of-body experience, it includes three case reports of near-death experiences in children. One child was two years and five months old at the time of his experience; another was four years old; and the third was about seven years old.

454. Gilbert, P. (1975). **Psychic children.** Psychic, 6(5), 16-19.

The article covers children's reactions to psychic experiences, research being conducted with children, personality characteristics affecting scoring, and type of psychic experiences encountered. Several noted parapsychologists are interviewed.

455. Guirdham, A. (1972). Obsession, psychic forces and evil in the causation of disease. London: Neville Spearman.

These are anecdotal cases with discussion of children who have obsessional symptoms, night terrors, psychic gifts, and memories of previous lives. The cases were treated by the author, who is a psychiatrist.

456. Hendricks, G. & Roberts, T. B. (1977). The second centering book. Englewood Cliffs, NJ: Prentice-Hall.

The book is written with an emphasis on children. It contains instructions for meditation, as well as instructions for helping parents and teachers work with children through fantasy, dreams, and intuition. A section devoted to parapsychology (pp. 157-197) briefly explains the field and the various types of phenomena; it includes exercises in telepathy, clairvoyance, precognition, and psychokinesis. An extensive alphabetical, topical bibliography is included.

457. Jones, C. (1989). From parent to child: The psychic link. NY: Warner Books.

This book focuses on the ESP link between parents and children from early pregnancy to infancy and childhood. The parents' perspective on psi phenomena is heavily drawn on, with research findings and anecdotal material added. There is a chapter on exercises to do during pregnancy or with your growing child, to help strengthen the ESP connection.

458. Moody, R. A. (1988). The Light Beyond. NY: Bantam Books.

This book, the latest book by Moody on the near-death experience, contains a chapter on children's NDE's. Many children visualize themselves as adults during the experience. Moody quotes extensively from accounts of three children, aged 9 to 11. He also discusses the findings of other researchers.

459. Peterson, J. W. (1987). The secret life of kids: An exploration into their psychic senses. Wheaton, IL: Theosophical Publishing House.

This book contains both theoretical and anecdotal material on children's psychic experiences. It includes an interview with Olga Worrall about her childhood and advice for teachers and parents. The author critiques "new age" spiritual practices for children.

460. Rogo, D. S. (1976). **A guide to juvenile literature on parapsychology.** Parapsychology Review, 7(3), 25-28.

This reviews books geared to younger readers (mainly junior high and high schoolers) interested in learning more about parapsychology.

461. Tanous, A. & Donnelly, K. F. (1979). Is your child psychic? NY: Macmillan Publishing Co. Reprinted as: Understanding and developing your child's natural psychic abilities: A guide for creative parents and teachers. NY: Simon & Schuster, 1988.

This book is designed to help parents and teachers understand children's psychic abilities. Such areas as telepathy, clairvoyance, precognition, color, imaginary playmates, out-of-body experiences, dreams, and personality types are covered. The final chapter covers game-like ESP tests to tap psychic abilities. The book contains numerous anecdotal reports.

462. Tralins, R. (1969). Children of the supernatural. NY: Lancer Books.

This is a compilation of anecdotes involving children who had psychic experiences (from dematerialization to telepathy). Reportedly, each case was verified as being true, although there is no indication of how thorough the investigations were.

463. Young, S. H. (1978). Psychic children. Garden City, NY: Doubleday.

This book has been written to help parents understand their child's psychic experiences. Spontaneous cases and anecdotal material cover telepathy, PK, precognition, and reincarnation. Alternative natural explanations for the psychic events are also offered. The final chapter focuses on how to deal with a psychic child and offers guidance to the parent.

Reviewed by: Drewes, A. A. (1977). Parapsychology Review, 8(4), 19-20.

APPENDIX A

GLOSSARY

AGENT: In a test of GESP, the individual who looks at the information constituting the target and who is said to "send" or "transmit" that information to a percipient; in a test of telepathy and in cases of spontaneous ESP, the individual about whose mental states information is acquired by a percipient. The term is sometimes used to refer to the subject in a test of PK.

CALL: (As noun), the overt response made by the percipient in guessing the target in a test of ESP; (as verb), to make a response.

CLAIRVOYANCE: Paranormal acquisition of information about an object or contemporary physical event; in contrast to telepathy, the information is assumed to derive directly from an external physical source and not from the mind of another person.

CLOSED DECK: A procedure for generating the target order for each run, not by independent random selection of successive targets, but by randomization of a fixed set of targets (e.g., a deck of 25 ESP cards containing exactly five of each of the standard symbols).

CONFIDENCE CALL: A response the subject feels relatively certain is correct and indicates so before it is compared with its target.

CRITICAL RATIO (CR): A mathematical quantity used to decide whether the size of the observed deviation from chance in a psi test is significantly greater than the expected degree of random fluctuation about the average: it is obtained by dividing by the standard deviation; also called the z statistic.
Critical Ratio of the Difference (CR_d): A critical ratio used to decide whether the numbers of hits obtained under two conditions (or by two groups of subjects) differ significantly from each other; it is obtained by dividing the difference

between the two total-hits scores by the standard deviation of the difference.

DECLINE EFFECT: The tendency for high scores in a test of psi to decrease, either within a run, within a session, or over a longer period of time; may also be used in reference to the waning and disappearance of psi talent.

DIFFERENTIAL EFFECT: In an experiment where the subjects are tested under two different procedural conditions: (i) the tendency of subjects who score above chance in one condition to score below chance in the other, and vice versa; (ii) the tendency of one condition to elicit psi-hitting from the group of subjects as a whole and the other condition to elicit psi-missing.

DISPLACEMENT: A form of ESP shown by a percipient who consistently obtains information about a target that is one or more removed, spatially or temporally, from the actual target designated for that trial.
Backward Displacement: Displacement in which the target extrasensorially cognized precedes the intended target by one, two, or more steps (designated as -1, -2, etc.).
Forward Displacement: Displacement in which the target actually responded to occurs later than the intended target by one, two, or more steps (designated as +1, +2, etc.).

ESP CARDS: Special cards, introduced by J. B. Rhine, for use in tests of ESP; a standard pack contains 25 cards, each portraying one of five symbols, viz., circle, cross, square, star, and waves.

EXPERIMENTER EFFECT: An experimental outcome that results, not from manipulation of the variable of interest itself, but from some aspect of the experimenter's behavior, such as unconscious communication to the subjects, or possibly even a psi-meditated effect working in accord with the experimenter's desire or motivation.

EXTRASENSORY PERCEPTION (ESP): Paranormal cognition; the acquisition of information about an external event, object, or influence (mental or physical, past, present, or future) in some way other than through any of the known sensory channels.

FORCED-CHOICE TEST: Any test of ESP in which the percipient is required to make a response that is limited to a range of possibilities known in advance.

FREE-RESPONSE TEST: Any test of ESP in which the range of possible targets is relatively unlimited and is unknown to the percipient, thus permitting a free response to whatever impressions come to mind.

GANZFELD: Term for a special type of environment (or the technique for producing it) consisting of homogeneous unpatterned sensory stimulation; an audiovisual ganzfeld may be accomplished by placing halved ping-pong balls over each eye of the subject, with diffused light (frequently red in hue) projected onto them from an external source, together with the playing of unstructured sounds (such as "pink noise") into the ears.

GENERAL EXTRASENSORY PERCEPTION (GESP): A noncommittal technical term used to refer to instances of ESP in which the information paranormally acquired may have derived either from another person's mind (i.e., as telepathy), or from a physical event or state of affairs (i.e., as clairvoyance), or even from both sources.

GOAL-ORIENTED: Term for the hypothesis that psi accomplishes a subject's or experimenter's objective as economically as possible, irrespective of the complexity of the physical system involved.

MACRO-PK: Any psychokinetic effect that does not require statistical analysis for its demonstration; sometimes used to refer to PK that has as its target a system larger than quantum mechanical processes, including microorganisms, dice, as well as larger objects.

MAJORITY-VOTE TECHNIQUE (MV): The so-called repeated or multiple-guessing technique of testing for ESP. The symbol most frequently called by a subject (or a group of subjects) for a given target is used as the "majority-vote" response to that target on the theory that such a response is more likely to be correct than one obtained from a single call.

MEAN CHANCE EXPECTATION (MCE): The average (or "mean") number of hits, or the most likely score to be expected in a test of psi on the null hypothesis that nothing apart from chance is involved in the production of the score.

MICRO-PK: Any psychokinetic effect that requires statistical analysis for its demonstration. Sometimes used to refer to PK that has as its target a quantum mechanical system.

OPEN DECK: A procedure for generating a target order in which each successive target is chosen at random independently of all the others; thus, for example, in the case of a standard deck of ESP cards whose target order is "open deck," each type of symbol is not necessarily represented an equal number of times.

OUT-OF-THE-BODY EXPERIENCE (OBE): An experience, either spontaneous or induced, in which one's center of consciousness seems to be in a spatial location outside of one's physical body.

PARANORMAL: Term for any phenomenon that in one or more respects exceeds the limits of what is deemed physically possible on current scientific assumptions.

PARAPSYCHOLOGY: The scientific study of certain paranormal or ostensibly paranormal phenomena, in particular, ESP and PK.

PERCIPIENT: The individual who experiences or "receives" an extrasensory influence or impression; also, one who is tested for ESP ability.

POLTERGEIST: A disturbance characterized by physical effects of ostensibly paranormal origin, suggesting mischievous or destructive intent. These phenomena include such events as the unexplained movement or breakage of objects, loud raps, electrical disturbances, and the lighting of fires.

POSITION EFFECT (PE): The tendency of scores in a test of psi to vary systematically according to the location of the trial on the record sheet.

PRECOGNITION: A form of ESP involving awareness of some future event that cannot be deduced from normally known data in the present.

PROCESS-ORIENTED: Term for research whose main objective is to determine how the occurrence of psi is related to other factors and variables.

PROOF-ORIENTED: Term for research whose main objective is to gain evidence for the existence of psi.

PSI: A general term used either as a noun or adjective to identify ESP or PK.

PSI-HITTING: The use of psi in such a way that the target at which the subject is aiming is "hit" (correctly responded to in a test of ESP, or influenced in a test of PK) more frequently than would be expected if only chance were operating.

PSI-MISSING: The use of psi in such a way that the target at which the subject is aiming is "missed" (responded to incorrectly in a test of ESP, or influenced in a direction contrary to aim in a test of PK) more frequently than would be expected if only chance were operating.

PSYCHOKINESIS (PK): Paranormal action; the influence of mind on a physical system that cannot be entirely accounted for by the mediation of any known physical energy.

RANDOM EVENT GENERATOR (REG): An apparatus (typically electronic) incorporating an element capable of generating a random sequence of outputs; used in automated tests of psi for generating target sequences; in tests of PK, it may itself be the target system that the subject is required to influence, also called a random number generator (RNG)

RECURRENT SPONTANEOUS PSYCHOKINESIS (RSPK): Expression for paranormal physical effects that occur repeatedly over a period of time; used especially as a technical term for poltergeist disturbances.

REMOTE VIEWING: A term for ESP used especially in the

context of an experimental design wherein a percipient attempts to describe the surroundings of a geographically distant agent.

RESPONSE BIAS: The tendency to respond or behave in predictable, nonrandom ways.

RETROACTIVE PK: PK producing an effect backward in time; to say that event A was caused by retroactive PK is to say that A would not have happened in the way that it did had it not been for a later PK effort exerted so as to influence it; sometimes abbreviated as retro-PK; also referred to as backward PK or time-displaced PK.

RUN: A fixed group of successive trials in a test of psi.

SHEEP-GOAT EFFECT (SGE): The relationship between one's acceptance of the possibility of ESP's occurrence under the given experimental conditions and the level of scoring actually achieved on that ESP test; specifically, the tendency for those who do not reject this possibility ("sheep") to score above chance and those who do reject it ("goats") to score below chance.

SPONTANEOUS CASE: Any psychic occurrence that takes place naturally, and often unanticipated, in a real-life situation, as opposed to the experimentally elicited psi phenomena of the laboratory.

STACKING EFFECT: A spuriously high (or low) score in a test of ESP when two or more percipients make guesses in relation to the same sequence of targets; it is due to a fortuitous relationship occurring between the guessing biases of the percipients and the peculiarities of the target sequence.

TARGET: In a test of ESP, the object or event that the percipient attempts to identify through information paranormally acquired; in a test of PK, the physical system, or a prescribed outcome thereof, that the subject attempts to influence or bring about.

TELEPATHY: The paranormal acquisition of information about the thoughts, feelings, or activity of another conscious being.

TRIAL: An experimentally defined smallest unit of measurement in a test of psi: in a test of ESP, it is usually associated with the attempt to gain information paranormally about a single target; in a test of PK, it is usually defined in terms of the single events to be influenced.

VARIANCE: A statistic for the degree to which a group of scores are scattered or dispersed around their average; formally, it is the average of the squared deviations from the mean; in parapsychology, the term is often used somewhat idiosyncratically to refer to the variance around the theoretical mean of a group of scores (e.g., MCE) rather than around the actual, obtained mean.

Run-Score Variance: The variance around the mean of the scores obtained on individual runs.

Subject Variance: The variance around the mean of a subject's total score.

Reprinted with permission of The Journal of Parapsychology. For an extended list, see Michael A. Thalbourne's A Glossary of Terms in Parapsychology, William Heinemann, Ltd., London, 1982.

APPENDIX B

SELECTED PARAPSYCHOLOGY RESEARCH AND RESOURCE CENTERS

AMERICAN SOCIETY FOR PSYCHICAL RESEARCH (ASPR)
5 West 73rd Street, New York, NY 10023
(212) 799-5050

Membership society. Publishes quarterly Journal of the American Society for Psychical Research and ASPR Newsletter, sponsors lectures, distributes introductory material, sells test materials and books. Reference library. Offers comprehensive listing of university and college classes, and programs in parapsychology ($6.00, postpaid).

FOUNDATION FOR RESEARCH ON THE NATURE OF MAN (FRNM), Institute for Parapsychology
P.O. Box 6847, College Station, Durham, NC 27708
(919) 688-8241

Conducts laboratory research on ESP and psychokinesis, publishes quarterly Journal of Parapsychology and FRNM Bulletin, distributes introductory information, sells test materials and books (list available on request). Reference library. Conducts annual, two-month Summer Study Program as well as residential Advanced Program in experimental parapsychology. Offers tours of research facilities each Thursday at 11:30 am, or by appointment. Thursday Research Meeting (noon) open to the public.

MIND SCIENCE FOUNDATION
8301 Broadway, Suite 100, San Antonio, TX 78209
(512) 821-6094

Conducts laboratory research on ESP and psychokinesis, sponsors seminars. Publishes newsletter, maintains reference library.

PARAPSYCHOLOGICAL ASSOCIATION, INC.
P.O. Box 12236, Research Triangle Park, NC 27707
(919) 688-8241

The professional parapsychology research organization. Member of the American Association for the Advancement of Science. Elects Members and Associate Members on the basis of their research; accepts interested Affiliates from other scholarly fields. Holds annual August convention, open to the public, at which research papers are presented; proceedings of convention (Research in Parapsychology) and newsletter are distributed to all dues-paying member categories listed above.

PARAPSYCHOLOGY FOUNDATION
228 East 71st Street, New York, NY 10021
(212) 628-1550

Houses the Eileen J. Garrett Library, which is open to public for reference only. Sponsors annual international parapsychological conferences and publishes their Proceedings Offers annually updated "Guide to Sources of Information on Parapsychology" ($1.00, enclose stamped, self-addressed business envelope).

PARAPSYCHOLOGY SOURCES OF INFORMATION (PSI) CENTER
2 Plane Tree Lane, Dix Hills, NY 11746
(516) 271-1243

Collects, catalogs, and indexes books, journals, and other resources dealing with parapsychology and transformation of consciousness. Computerized parapsychological database. Fee-based services include: research consultation (by contract), answers to specific research questions, comprehensive bibliographies on topic(s) of your choice. Publishes Parapsychology Abstracts International, now called Exceptional Human Experience (broader in scope), numerous bibliographies and reference works. Sells secondhand books and journals (list available for $3.00). Phone between 9:00 am and 3:00 pm EST, Monday through Friday.

SOCIETY FOR PSYCHICAL RESEARCH (SPR)
1 Adam and Eve Mews, London W8 6UG, England, U.K.
(071) 937-8984

Membership society. Founded in 1882, it is the oldest organization devoted to investigating paranormal phenomena. Publishes its Proceedings, Journal, and Newsletter Sponsors lectures and distributes introductory material. Reference library.

DEGREE PROGRAMS

Many people who ask about parapsychological education are considering careers in this field. Because career opportunities in parapsychology are so limited, very few colleges and universities offer degree programs in it. None offers a B.A. or B.S. program. At the graduate level, a few institutions provide students with the opportunity to specialize in parapsychology.

The only university at which students may earn a degree expressly in parapsychology (that is, a parapsychology degree) is ANDHRA UNIVERSITY (Department of Psychology and Parapsychology, Visakhapatnam 530 003, India). Students enrolled in this 3-year Ph.D. program may conduct their research and prepare their dissertations either at Andhra (where the affiliated Institute for Yoga and Consciousness, in addition to the department, sponsors psi research) or at the FRNM.

Specialization in parapsychology is an option for students enrolled in the psychology Ph.D. program at the UNIVERSITY OF EDINBURGH (Department of Psychology, 7 George Square, Edinburgh EH8 9JZ, Scotland), where Dr. Robert L. Morris, Koestler Professor of Parapsychology, directs an active laboratory psi research program. Graduate students in both the human sciences and psychology programs at SAYBROOK INSTITUTE (1550 Sutter Street, San Francisco, CA 94109, Dr. Stanley Krippner, Director) may also specialize in parapsychology. The interdisciplinary consciousness studies program (Master's) at JOHN F. KENNEDY UNIVERSITY (12 Altarinda Road, Orinda, CA 94563) includes parapsychological instruction. Also, specialized classes and research supervision enable students pursuing the M.A. in psychology at WEST GEORGIA COLLEGE (Department of Psychology, Carrollton, GA 30118) to emphasize parapsychology in their studies.

OTHER ACCREDITED STUDY

A number of other colleges and universities offer for-credit, elective parapsychology classes at both the undergraduate and graduate levels (and note that many will grant credit hours for FRNM's SSP). Some of these (where, for example, research parapsychologists are faculty members in psychology or other departments) additionally provide excellent opportunities for accredited, independent study of the field. The AMERICAN SOCIETY FOR PSYCHICAL RESEARCH (5 West 73rd Street, New York, NY 10023) maintains a comprehensive, annotated listing of such educational opportunities, which may be purchased for $6.00 (US, postpaid, please enclose stamped, self-addressed, business envelope).

Material in Appendix B drawn from lists compiled and distributed by the Foundation for Research on the Nature of Man.

INDEX OF AUTHORS

Number(s) following author's name indicate sequential position in the bibliography.

ABOUT THE AUTHORS

Athena A. Drewes (M.A. Clinical Psychology, New York University; M.S. and Psy.D. doctoral candidate, School Psychology, Pace University) is a child psychotherapist, school psychologist, and researcher in New York. She has been an elected member of the Parapsychological Association for 14 years, was Managing Editor of its Bulletin Psi News for five years, and has written numerous articles and reviews as well as lectured on parapsychology. Ms. Drewes lives in Washingtonville, New York, with her husband, Jim Bridges, and two sons, Scott and Seth.

Sally Ann Drucker (Ph.D. English, State University of New York at Buffalo) has been an elected member of the Parapsychological Association for 14 years; she was an Associate Editor of its Bulletin, Psi News, for five years. Dr. Drucker has written numerous parapsychology research reports, articles, and reviews; she has also taught classes, presented workshops and lectures, and made media appearances in the field. She is currently a consultant at the Foundation for Research on the Nature of Man/Institute for Parapsychology in Durham, North Carolina, where she edits their newsletter.

In the 1970s, while affiliated with the Maimonides Medical Center's Division of Parapsychology and Psychophysics, both authors focused their research on children's ESP. Their work has appeared, among other places, in the Journal of the American Society for Psychical Research and Research in Parapsychology (Scarecrow Press).